A COMPLICATED
PREGNANCY

A COMPLICATED PREGNANCY

WHETHER MARY WAS A VIRGIN AND WHY IT MATTERS

KYLE ROBERTS

FORTRESS PRESS

MINNEAPOLIS

A COMPLICATED PREGNANCY

Whether Mary Was a Virgin and Why It Matters

All subsequent Bible references, unless otherwise noted, are to the *New
Revised Standard Version.*

Cover image: Leighton Connor

Cover design: Brad Norr

Print ISBN: 978-1-5064-0624-4

eBook ISBN: 978-1-5064-0625-1

The paper used in this publication meets the minimum requirements of
American National Standard for Information Sciences — Permanence of
Paper for Printed Library Materials, ANSI Z329.48-1984.

Manufactured in the U.S.A.

This book was produced using Pressbooks.com, and PDF rendering was done
by PrinceXML.

For my mom,
Nancy Louise Roberts
(1946–2015)

CONTENTS

Introduction: "Don't Mess with My Manger Scene!" ix

1. Beautiful Blood 1

2. What's So Bad about Good Sex? 29

3. Virgin Births Happen to Sharks, but Not to Humans 57

4. The Most Powerful Woman in the World 83

5. A Controversial and Too-Silent Night 109

6. How Not to Lose Your Baby Jesus 137

7. God's Deep Dive into Creation 159

Conclusion: A More Human God 190
Acknowledgments 203

INTRODUCTION: "DON'T MESS WITH MY MANGER SCENE!"

A package arrived from Aunt Jenny. My mom sat by the kitchen table and carefully tore back the brown, crumpled paper. It was a crèche from the Dominican Republic, where my aunt had recently moved. Out popped Jesus and Mary, a few shepherds, and the three wise men (the Bible doesn't specify there were three, but no matter). Digging further into the package led to a gruesome but bloodless discovery: Joseph had been decapitated in transit.

Mom collected manger scenes from all over the world. My parents traveled a lot over the years, due to my dad's role on an international mission board and then as a pastor for nearly a decade in Europe. Wherever they traveled, she acquired a locally handcrafted manger scene. Her collection continued to expand as other friends and family members, including Aunt Jenny, got in on the action.

Mom liked to remember the distinct local cultures, and she loved what the manger scene signifies. The birth of Jesus marks the entrance of the eternal Son of God into our beautiful, messy, and multicultural world. Every Thanksgiving, she pulled out those manger scenes and placed them around the house. More unfortunate accidents and the occasional mystery occurred: one year, baby Jesus just up and disappeared from the Kenyan set. We prayed to the Good Lord and hoped to high heaven that Phoebe, our cranky Lhasa Apso, hadn't swallowed the Son of God. Mom's infectious love for Christmas was channeled through the crèches.

In the summer of 2015, my mom died from the complications of Alzheimer's. Those manger scenes preserve our memory of her interest in global cultures and, even more, of her love for the meaning of Jesus's birth.

Each December offers new opportunities to read, hear, and enact the Christmas story. We remember the stories of Jesus's birth in song, sermons, drama, and manger scenes. Christians all over the world gaze upon images of Mary with the swaddled child. For throngs of the faithful, it rings true and warms the soul—the birth of the Son of God in the most mundane of places; not much fanfare; a small and undignified band of onlookers. The night and the birth that changed the world. While the cross and empty tomb are the lifeblood of Easter, the manger scene is the heart of Christmas. Like the cross and the tomb, it's a universal and sacred Christian symbol.

Conflicts of all sorts, whether political, religious, or ideological, involve disagreements about what counts as sacred.[1] Arguments about politics and religion, big government or small government, free will or divine sovereignty. Disputes about rights and freedoms, policy battles, and heated theological arguments. The sacred appears in symbols, images, pictures, and stories that lie just beyond the reach of critical examination. Dive deep into sacred territory and you'll understand the complicated and intense nature of our political and theological battles. There you'll find the source of vibrancy and conviction, but also of conflict and even war. For so many Christians, the manger scene—and what it signifies—is sacred.

THE ARGUMENT OF THE MONTH CLUB

In 2010 I found myself in the musty basement of a timeworn Catholic church in St. Paul, Minnesota. I'd been invited to debate the doctrine of Scripture's authority. Over 300 old-school Catholics crammed into that sweaty basement, and I was clearly the visiting team. They call themselves the "Argument of the Month Club." Playing the Protestant role, I argued for the doctrine of "Sola Scriptura," the Bible as primary authority for the Christian life and doctrine. I was fully aware that many Catholics think Protestants underemphasize and even belittle the significance of Mary, and that's not untrue. At one point during the debate, I made an impassioned plea that I, too, respect Mary as an important figure in the story of salvation and in the life of the church. That simple point bought me a good bit of traction with the crowd; they let out a collective sigh of appreciation.

Jesus was their savior, but Mary was their mother, and you don't mess with Mom. Other than Jesus, no other person in the Christian canon occupies as important a place in the spiritual and religious lives of believers.

From the early days of Christianity, the virgin birth has been held as a sacred doctrine. Theologians Irenaeus and Tertullian both mentioned the virgin birth within their summaries of the main tenets of Christianity, which they called a "Rule of Faith." Statements like these laid the foundation for the later creeds, summaries of theological beliefs deemed central to orthodoxy. From 381 CE onward, the main ecumenical creeds all include a reference to the virgin birth. And the Apostles' Creed (date unknown), recited in countless churches over the ages, declares that Jesus was "born of the Virgin Mary."

Belief in the virgin birth was a main theme in the controversy between conservative and liberal Protestants in the early 1900s. The self-proclaimed "fundamentalists" made it the first point in their two-volume series of essays defending orthodox Christianity against the encroachment of liberal heresy. Today, search the statement of faith of any evangelical or conservative Christian denomination, college, seminary, or parachurch organization, and you will likely find an affirmation of the virgin birth.

I should know. I was born and bred in the evangelical church.

COME, JOURNEY WITH ME

I was a PK (Preacher's Kid). My dad was a Southern Baptist pastor. So was my grandfather. Church was in my blood—Christianity was in my DNA. At nine years of age, I "accepted Jesus Christ as my Lord and Savior" and my father baptized me in short order.

We went to church on Sunday morning, Sunday evening, and Wednesday evening. We even sprinkled in the occasional Monday-night door-to-door evangelism or prayer gathering. Then came youth group and all the camps, Bible studies, and sexual purity talks (more about those later).

I attended a Southern Baptist seminary and then an evangelical divinity school for my doctorate in theology. When I graduated with my PhD in 2006, I was a bona fide evangelical theologian and I had the paper to prove it! But over the past decade I've slowly and steadily shifted away from my conservative roots, toward a more liberal theology. My vocation as a theologian challenged me in ways I couldn't have anticipated.

As I prepared lectures and engaged diverse and curious students, my theology expanded and grew. I read more broadly, engaging perspectives outside of the evangelical mainstream. I imbibed theologies of liberation and social justice; I became attuned to the ways that dominant Euro-American (i.e., white male) theologies contribute to the oppression of marginalized and vulnerable people. I had long ago ceased believing in a literal six-day, twenty-four-hour creation. But through my work as a professor and scholar, I started taking science even more seriously in my interpretation of the Bible. I accepted evolution as the way in which God created the world and human life. I left behind the evangelical doctrine of the Bible's "inerrancy" (complete truthfulness in every matter), though still affirming the Bible's authority for faith and discipleship. I embraced a more nuanced view of Christ's atoning death on the cross. I understood salvation as relating much more to this present life and more connected to our planet—and less about acquiring a passport to heaven after death. I began to sense that God's grace might be far more expansive than I ever realized. I adopted an inclusive view of sexuality in the church and a more ecumenical understanding of Christianity. I became less concerned with converting people to my way of Christianity and more passionate about living like Jesus in the world.

But while my theology shifted leftward, many of my core beliefs remain planted in my heart and mind. I still profess that God is Trinity. I still believe that Jesus was and is both fully divine and fully human. I still affirm the resurrection of Jesus and I hope in the promise of resurrection for the redemption of the world and for the entire cosmos.

And for me, the manger scene still matters.

That's why I've written this book.

I'm a progressive, Protestant Christian, but I still bear marks of my evangelical upbringing. I'm comfortable with phrases like *mere orthodoxy* and *big tent Christianity*. But I'm certainly no radical; I respect the weight of tradition and the emotional issues involved with questioning core beliefs. The question of the virgin birth is far more than a theological curiosity; it's an emotional and spiritual issue. The virgin birth matters for how people relate to God, for what they believe about Jesus and Mary, and for how they understand their own humanity. It has vast implications for how they understand the very nature of Christianity itself—and for how they practice it.

I know that for many of you, the manger scene is sacred, too. As I speak on this topic to church groups and in other contexts, I can often sense a palpable anxiety rising—sometimes in my audience, sometimes within me. I can imagine my mother, lovingly but firmly whispering in my ear, "Son, don't mess with my manger scene!"

I don't relish the thought of messing with anyone's manger scene, but I want to follow truth where it leads. The question of the virgin birth embarks us on a spiritual and theological journey. The port of departure is a simple question: *Was Jesus really born of a virgin?* And, if not, what does that mean for my faith? For yours?

I invite you to journey with me as we dig deep

into the manger scene and discover whether Jesus was really born of a virgin—and why that matters.

The Virgin Birth in a Coffee Shop

Not long ago, I plopped down in my favorite coffee shop to work on this book. I overheard two college students discussing religion. The young man laid out a series of popular skeptical arguments against Christianity and against religion in general. Religion is an opiate for the masses! Christianity is mythology, like every other religion! The Bible is an ancient, sexist, and severely flawed book! And so on. The young woman employed her basic apologetic training, listening patiently to his skeptical arguments and defending his charges with bits and pieces of arguments she'd learned in youth group or in sermons.

My ears perked up when they got to the topic of the virgin birth.

The skeptic explained that he had just seen a daytime talk show in which a twenty-something woman claimed to be the recipient of a miracle. She was pregnant—but she claimed to be a virgin. A modern Mary!

"Look," he said. "This woman was obviously

blaming God for something she did. Isn't this what's really going on with the virgin birth story? An elaborate cover-up for an indiscretion? You know, so Mary wouldn't get stoned for her crime."

He went on, as if he had her on the ropes.

"And what about all those other famous dudes in history that supposedly had miraculous births? Caesar Augustus, Plato, Alexander the Great! Why should we believe the Jesus version? And look at all the contradictions in the Gospel stories: you'd think they'd get their story straight. Why didn't they check with each other before writing this stuff down?"

The Christian countered as best she could: "But those stories are fundamentally different from the birth of Jesus. And the virgin birth is in the Bible. The Bible is God's perfect revelation. We need to accept and believe this miracle came from God. There may be some minor difficulties or even *apparent* contradictions, but that just means we have to—no, we *get to*—exercise faith."

At the next lull in their theology debate, I made my way over to the couple and invited myself into their conversation. I asked the skeptical atheist, "Would you find Christianity more compelling if you didn't need to believe in a literal virgin birth to be a Christian?"

"No," he quickly answered. "It wouldn't change

anything. There's all that crazy Old Testament stuff, too . . ."

Then I turned to the Christian apologist: "Do you think people need to believe in the virgin birth to consider themselves faithful Christians?"

"Absolutely," she said. "The virgin birth is essential to our understanding of Jesus Christ. If we don't accept *everything* that's true about him, then we lose everything."

These two evangelists—one for Christianity and the other for atheism—represent ends of a spectrum, drastically opposite answers to a very complicated question. They illustrate the tensions many people feel when they encounter the manger scene and the question of the virgin birth. But they also illustrate why it matters. It matters for our faith, for our understanding of God, and for how we practice Christianity in the world today.

Who is right? The skeptic or the believer? Or neither?

During a recent Christmas season, my questions about the virgin birth turned from being two-dimensional, at the level of speculative concepts, to a vivid three-dimensional experience. I sat in church week after week, singing songs that referenced the virgin Mary and the virgin birth, and I recited the Apostles' Creed. The questions behind this book hovered over me, forcing me to consider whether those songs and those creeds match my own beliefs.

Was Jesus really born of a virgin? Does it matter?

The answer to that question leads us to another place, at once deeper and broader: it leads us to a theology of the incarnation. And that's what this book has become: a journey through a complicated but foundational assertion about who Jesus really was—and is. Throughout this journey, we'll discover anew the significance of the coming of God in the flesh. The presence of God in human history. From its emergence in the Gospels, the virgin birth pronounces that Jesus came from God and that he was a true, real, human being, like you and me. But what does the story of the virgin birth mean for us today? And should we still believe it?

THE BARE-BONES VIRGIN BIRTH IN THE BIBLICAL GOSPELS

Until the Enlightenment, most Christian theologians took the historicity of the virgin birth of Jesus for granted. They assumed Jesus was miraculously conceived by the Holy Spirit in Mary, who was a virgin at the time of the conception. This assumption is mainly based on the two Gospels that tell us about Jesus's birth: Matthew and Luke.

Matthew provides little detail about the miraculous conception, telling us matter-of-factly that Mary was "engaged to Joseph, but before they lived together, she was found to be with child from the Holy Spirit" (Matthew 1:18). An angel responds to Joseph's alarm with an assurance that "the child conceived in her is from the Holy Spirit" (Matthew 1:20) and is Jesus, the one who will save the people from their sins. Connecting Jesus's birth to Israel's expectation of a Messiah, the story includes a reference to Isaiah 7:14: "Look, the virgin shall conceive and bear a son, and they shall name him Emmanuel," which means, "God is with us" (Matthew 1:23). But few details are provided about the nature of the conception itself. Matthew indicates that Mary's pregnancy was a miraculous work of God. The main point of Matthew's infancy narrative is that God had broken into the world in a new way to bring long-awaited salvation for Israel: Jesus is God's presence with us; he is Emmanuel.

Luke is more explicit about Mary's virginity. He also gives the name of the angel, Gabriel, who appears to Mary. Luke describes Mary as a virgin engaged to be married (Luke 1:27). In this story, the angel delivers the news to Mary *prior* to the pregnancy. She's told that she will conceive a child who will be "Son of the Most High" (Luke 1:31). When

Mary questions the angel's proclamation, pointing out the obvious problem (that she is a virgin, for goodness sake!), the angel explains that the "Holy Spirit will come upon you, and the power of the Most High will overshadow you" (Luke 1:35). She will bear a child—and that child will be the Messiah and savior.

That's about it. There are more details about the before and the after of the birth, but we aren't given much information, either about Mary's miraculous pregnancy or about the birth itself. In Luke, after the couple travels to Bethlehem for the census, we're told that "she gave birth to her firstborn son and wrapped him in bands of cloth, and laid him in a manger, because there was no place for them in the inn" (Luke 2:7). The birth itself appears unremarkable. Matthew is even more subtle, telling us that after Joseph heard the news from the angel, he "took her as his wife but had no marital relations with her until she had borne a son; and he named him Jesus" (Matthew 1:24–25).

The two Gospels do not provide many details about the virginity of Mary, the conception by the Holy Spirit, or the nature of the birth itself. But that hasn't prevented theologians from speculating about those topics and what they might mean for us.

And speculate they did.

NOTES

1. For a discussion of how sacredness factors into political and religious debates in the U.S., see Jonathan Haidt's *The Righteous Mind: Why Good People Are Divided by Politics and Religion* (New York: Vintage, 2013). Also see Bill Moyers's interview with Haidt at http://billmoyers.com/segment/jonathan-haidt-explains-our-contentious-culture/.

1

BEAUTIFUL BLOOD

I'm not a fan of blood. Don't get me wrong: I understand its importance. But like most people, I prefer to keep it under my skin. I'm squeamish when a nurse pokes my arm, and I won't look at the needle. I learned early on that the medical profession wasn't for me.

Ella, our first child, was born on March 28, 2010. It was a difficult pregnancy for my wife, Sara. As nervous first-time parents, Sara and I went through all the preparations. We'd taken the classes, and we'd done the homework. We'd heard again and again that even pregnancies that result in healthy babies and healthy moms never turn out exactly as you expect or as you envision in your dreams. And we learned that is true.

For Sara, morning sickness turned out to be morning, afternoon, and evening sickness, and lasted through the entire term of her pregnancy. When the time finally came, Sara was more than ready for our baby to make her way into the world. When we arrived at the hospital, the nurse informed us that Sara was nine centimeters dilated. After commending Sara for waiting it out at home until just the right time, she predicted a quick labor. But that didn't happen.

Instead, Sara labored for over twelve hours, through the evening and into the early hours of the morning. When Ella finally made her entrance into the world, I felt an incredible sense of relief and happiness: relief for Sara that the hard pregnancy was over and happiness for the long-anticipated arrival of this precious bundle of energy with flapping arms.

I also remember the blood. It seems like there was blood everywhere. Blood on the bed, blood on the medical instruments, blood on the floor. Blood on the doctor, the nurses, my wife, our baby. But the weird thing was, everyone was smiling and happy. It's a strange sensation to see so much smiling and to feel so much joy, and for those smiles and that joy to be around so much blood. I recall a sudden flash of amazement that the blood didn't bother me at all.

The blood symbolized new life. Birth makes blood beautiful.

The New Testament's two Gospel infancy narratives (Matthew and Luke) both testify to a virginal *conception*, though not explicitly to a virgin birth. Today, when most people refer to the virgin birth, they really mean the virginal conception—the Holy Spirit supernaturally conceived the zygote Jesus in Mary without the participation of a male human (namely, Joseph). But in the early church, the virgin birth took on another layer of meaning.

Most people haven't even heard of the antiquarian but spirited debates about whether Mary technically remained a virgin during—and after—the delivery of the infant Jesus. Some early theologians insisted that when the baby Jesus passed through Mary's birth canal, her hymen wasn't ruptured. In other words, there was no bloody, painful birth. She could have kept her legs crossed and the baby Jesus still would have appeared! The miraculous conception wasn't enough; they needed a miraculous delivery too.

They tried to sanitize Jesus's birth. Maybe they, too, were squeamish about blood and birth. These interpretations have informed many Christians' views of Mary ever since. They've also shaped the way Christians think about birth, sex, and blood.

But the insistence upon a virginal birth—a painless and bloodless delivery of baby Jesus—came at a heavy theological cost: it undermined the point of the incarnation.

MARY'S PAINLESS PREGNANCY AND JESUS'S BLOODLESS BIRTH

Valentinus (100–160 CE) was the most famous Gnostic theologian in the early church. He founded his own school, imbuing his followers with secret knowledge (*gnosis*) through which they could escape the lowly confines of their bodies and ascend to the spiritual plane. He viewed the human body as a trap out of which the soul needs to escape. He devalued the physical world: Who needs matter when you can have spirit? Valentinus couldn't countenance the notion that God would be truly embodied in the person of Jesus Christ. For him, God only *appeared* to be a human in Jesus.

The Gnostic impulse to deny the physical world and elevate the spiritual or immaterial lies behind Docetism, an ancient theology that taught Jesus was not a true human being. Docetists said the Son of God took on the appearance of a man in the form of Jesus, but he was a phantasm, a ghost, a mirage. The human form of Jesus was illusory. (Think of Princess

Leia's hologram, but more realistic and life-sized.) Docetists argued that God, in the form of Jesus, didn't suffer and die on the cross; the crucifixion didn't really happen to a human body.

The early church denounced Docetism as heresy. For Christian theologians, the incarnation means that the Son of God truly became a human being. God "in-fleshes" in the person Jesus of Nazareth. For them, Mary had a crucial role in the incarnation. Along with offering her womb, she provided the Son of God the physical material (flesh) necessary to be born Jesus of Nazareth. The virgin birth meant that Jesus was a true human being, because he was born of a human mother (*born of a woman*).

Yet not all orthodox theologians agreed on how the incarnation plays out with respect to the birth of Jesus. (Take note: Theological argument isn't a recent invention—it's been a popular hobby since the very beginning of Christianity!) Some theologians sounded downright gnostic when they discussed Mary and the virgin birth. Despite their insistence that Jesus was fully human, they couldn't quite overcome their suspicion of the human body. They couldn't countenance the fleshy, fluid-filled reality of human birth: a messy, bloody, painful, and beautiful endeavor. For them, Jesus's birth was nothing like when my Ella was born, with beautiful blood everywhere.

THE HOLY HYMEN

Consider, for example, the early church father Ambrose (337–397 CE) who links the "gate of the sanctuary" of the temple in Jerusalem (Ezekiel 44:1–2) to Mary's hymen: "Holy Mary is the gate of which it is written: 'The Lord will pass through it, and it will be shut,' after birth, for as a virgin she conceived and gave birth."[1] Ambrose elaborates that no man "shall pass through" that gate (Mary's hymen) except for God. In another text, he insists that Jesus "preserved the fence of her chastity and the inviolate seal of her virginity."[2]

Or his student Augustine (354–430 CE) who argues that because the resurrected Jesus could walk through walls, it's no stretch (no pun intended) to believe that the baby Jesus could pass through the "closed doors" of Mary's vagina without disturbing the hymen.[3] The laws of physics and of biology do not apply to the birth of the Son of God. Augustine ends this segment with a dramatic portrayal of the delivery of baby Jesus: "As an infant He came forth, a spouse from His bride-chamber, that is, from the virginal womb, leaving His Mother's integrity inviolate."[4]

I must admit: I never read those passages in seminary!

They weren't the first theologians to insist that the birth of Jesus was a painless and bloodless one, leaving Mary's hymen intact. Irenaeus (130–202 CE) and Clement of Alexandria (150–215 CE) taught that there was no biological disruption in Mary's body nor was there any physical travail during the birth of Jesus.[5] As strange as this may sound to us, they had their theological reasons for preserving Mary's body throughout the delivery—and for protecting the baby Jesus from the physicality of birth.

The story of the "Fall" of Adam and Eve (Genesis 3:16), their disobedience to God which resulted in devastating consequences, is told and retold in churches across the globe. The curse of Adam meant that men would forever work the land with difficulty and frustration; for women, the curse of Eve meant pain in childbirth. For Ambrose, the painless, bloodless virginal birth reversed this curse. Mary, the "new Eve," experienced no pain while birthing Jesus, and this illustrated that salvation had arrived. But the beauty in that *reverse the curse* theology pales in comparison to the problems that come with a sanitized, painless birth of Jesus.

The assumption that Mary's hymen was undisturbed by the birth of Jesus didn't originate with the Gospels of Matthew and Luke, both of which are sparse in delivery-room detail, but from texts dating to the middle of the first and early second centuries (CE). These texts are often called *apocryphal* texts. The name derives from a Greek word meaning "hidden," suggesting the texts should be hidden because they aren't worthy of being introduced to the public and used in Christian worship and teaching. More generally, the name implies they contain hidden or mysterious elements.[6]

Although these apocryphal books never rose to the level of New Testament canon, they nevertheless exerted a great deal of influence on early Christian theology and liturgy. Even today, Catholics include the main fifteen apocryphal texts in their Bibles. Many Protestants look askance at them. I recall the first time I discovered their existence when I flipped through the *New Oxford Annotated Bible* for a seminary class.[7] It was an odd experience seeing books like Sirach, Susanna, and Bel and the Dragon in my Bible.

The apocryphal infancy narratives inspired a lot of Christian reflection on the virgin birth. They didn't make it into the big-league list of fifteen, but they shaped subsequent beliefs about Mary and the virgin birth. The *Ascension of Isaiah* is an early Christian compilation of stories about the prophet Isaiah and about Jesus, and includes a brief narrative of his birth. This is the earliest known text that suggests the idea that Mary remained a virgin during the birth of Jesus (virginity *in partu*, or during the birth).[8] In that story, the baby Jesus magically appears outside the womb to Mary and Joseph, after only two months of pregnancy (I just mentioned this to Sara, my wife, and she said that sounds just fine to her).

The notion continues in another early Christian collection, the *Odes of Solomon*, which indicates that Mary experienced no labor pain. But the idea of virginity *during the birth* is most fully developed in the *Gospel of James* (also known as the *Protoevangelium of James*), a text that has been influential on theologians' views of Mary, and on the entire field of Mariology.[9] It provided the basis for the idea of Mary's "perpetual virginity," the belief that Mary remained a virgin throughout her life.

UNLESS I THRUST IN MY FINGER, I WILL NOT BELIEVE!

The *Gospel of James* gives us a backstory of the birth of Jesus by narrating Mary's birth and early life. It introduces Mary's parents, Anna and Joachim, and their devotion to the Lord. Anna prayed fervently to God to open her barren womb to give birth to a child. The story has obvious resonance with the Old Testament story of Hannah and her appeal to God to provide her with a child. Her prayer results in the birth of Samuel and of Hannah's dedication of him in the temple (1 Samuel 1–2:10). In a similar way, Anna and Joachim dedicate their daughter Mary to the temple at only three years of age, where she learns the path of holiness and religious devotion. Her youthful dedication to God prepares her for her unique blessing as the one who would give birth to Jesus.

The story goes on to say that when Mary reached marriageable age (approximately twelve years old), the priests hastened to find her a husband "lest perchance she defile the sanctuary of the Lord" through ritual uncleanliness—in other words, menstruation. Suitors from the region were invited to compete for the bride, and the significantly older Joseph, a widower with children of his own, was chosen from among the candidates. A dove flew out of his rod and landed on his head, an ancient, biblical version of the sorting hat. Joseph reluctantly accepted the call to take the young Mary into his household. He had to leave home to travel on business, but promised to marry her upon his return.

During his absence, Mary was informed by an angel that she would conceive. Her pregnancy caused a stir among the religious power brokers: the priests who learned of her apparent indiscretion and Joseph's illicit behavior were enraged at the betrothed couple's impropriety and disobedience. Both Mary and Joseph were proven innocent through a ritual resembling a witch-trial. When God apparently protected them from harm, the priests were finally convinced of their innocence.

Mary gave birth to Jesus in a cave underneath a "luminous cloud." A blinding light covered her. When it dissipated, the newly born Jesus was revealed and he immediately latched onto the breast of his mother. The midwife, who played no effective role in the delivery, proclaimed to another midwife, Salome: "I have a strange sight to relate to you: a virgin has brought forth—a thing which her nature admits not of." Then said Salome: "As the Lord my God lives, unless I thrust in my finger, and search the parts, I will not believe that a virgin has brought forth."

Salome, this story's version of a doubting Thomas, investigated Mary's vagina to prove that this miracle had really occurred; sure enough, Mary was still a virgin. Her doubts were met by a burning sensation in her hand, as she exclaimed: "My hand is dropping off as if burned with fire."

This story formed the basis of subsequent assumptions about Mary's virginity; her sexual purity had been preserved and her feminine body protected through the miraculous, cloud-covered birth of Jesus. This influence was unfortunate, however, because it allowed docetic tendencies to creep in to the way theologians read the two Gospel accounts of Jesus's birth. If we take the incarnation seriously, we should embrace the biological realities of birth, not deny them.

Could Baby Jesus Have Suffered from Meconium Aspiration Syndrome?

We had a minor scare when our second child, Luke, was born. His first two weeks of life were challenging because during his exit from the birth canal, he inhaled some pretty nasty stuff—a combination of amniotic fluid and his own feces. He had a pretty bad case of Meconium Aspiration Syndrome, which, while not uncommon, can be dangerous. His delicate first two weeks of life were spent in the hospital hooked up to oxygen, learning to breathe and cleansing his system. We were about to take him home with oxygen supply when suddenly he took a turn for the better. We breathed a big sigh of relief, grateful to bring home a healthy, if not always happy, baby.

If we accept the logic of some early theologians, the infant Jesus was immune to Meconium Aspiration Syndrome. Jesus's birth was, for them, supernaturally sanitized and protected from the messiness of normal, human birth. A miraculous conception wasn't enough: he needed to be miraculously delivered, too—unsullied by the biological fluids and substances endemic to human birth.

This sanitized version of the birth of Jesus creates a nasty theological mess.

While I can't say that the infant Jesus *did* experience anything like Meconium Aspiration Syndrome, I insist on the possibility. From his birth to his death, the fully human Jesus would have experienced illness, disease, and tragedy of one sort or other. To be human is to be exposed to the elements of nature and of biology. Bodily fluid, blood, feces, urine, saliva, semen, milk; as undignified and disgusting as these elements of human nature appear to us at times, they are essential aspects of *us*. They signal life, vitality, and struggle.

Thankfully, some theologians disagreed with this sterilized notion of Mary's virginity *during the birth.* While they affirmed a miraculous, supernatural conception, they argued that the theology of incarnation calls for a normal biological delivery. Jesus was truly and fully human, so his birth must have been fully human, too. To sanitize and spiritualize Jesus's entrance into the world undermines the goodness of creation and of human life.

The North African theologian Tertullian (160–220 CE) viewed the birth of Jesus as a fulfillment of Exodus 13:2, which reads, "Consecrate to me all the firstborn; whatever is the first to open the womb among the Israelites, of human beings and animals, is mine." He saw in this verse a reference to the physical opening of Mary's womb—and therefore to a natural, physical delivery of the baby Jesus.[10]

An obscure theologian, Helvidius (exact dates unknown), had argued against the notion that Mary's hymen remained intact during the birth of Jesus. For Helvidius, affirmation of the virginity of Mary *during the birth* and *after the birth* of Jesus constitutes a rejection of the theology of incarnation and reveals an insufficient appreciation for the goodness of creation.[11] We're aware of his arguments only because of more prominent theologians like Jerome (347–420 CE), who wrote an essay arguing against Helvidius. In that essay, Jerome extolled the merits of lifelong chastity, based on the example of Mary's preserved virginity.

Jovinian (exact dates unknown), a fourth-century monk, also opposed the idea of a sanitized and spiritualized virginal delivery. Like everyone else, he affirmed the virginal conception. But he argued that a true theology of the incarnation necessitated that the birth of Jesus be a normal, biological event. Otherwise, you're left with a phantom Jesus. And how can a phantom save us?

We're far from arriving at an answer to our main question, *whether Jesus was really born of a virgin?* But at this early stage in our journey, let's affirm this: Jesus wasn't a disembodied spirit. He was a real, flesh, bone, blood, and brain human being. And his birth reflected his genuine humanity. In other words, Jesus could have suffered from Meconium Aspiration Syndrome.

THE ICKY, STICKY, STINKY BODY OF THE DIVINE SON OF GOD

The gnostic Valentinus suggested that Jesus "ate and drank in a special way, without evacuating food. So great was his power of continence that the food was not corrupted in him."[12] Now that just seems crazy. But for Valentinus and other gnostic thinkers, Jesus never needed a bathroom break because he didn't poop. How could he, if he was God? Valentinus's aversion to a defecating Son of God amounts to a non-incarnational theology.

The embodied life of Jesus affirms the icky, sticky, stinky stuff of the human body. The Son of God really experienced a bodily, human life.

Human beings inherit and learn the impulse of disgust. We instinctively avoid some things and are socialized to avoid other things. When natural elements of the body are part of us, they are clean. When they are separated from us they become external or "other," rendered unclean and repulsive.

A famous psychology experiment provides insight into the "disgust impulse."[13] People have no problem swallowing their saliva so long as it remains inside their mouths. We can feel it with our tongues, even swish it about, and gulp it down. We do it unconsciously most of the time. But our saliva becomes "spit" once it's expelled from our bodies. Spit into a Dixie cup, then drink it: you've got the idea. When it's inside our bodies, it's clean; when it's outside our bodies, it's disgusting. Our disgust impulse creates psychological boundaries between what is clean and unclean, appealing and appalling.

Richard Beck suggests that the Eucharist, the Lord's Supper, is an ingenious liturgical practice precisely because it involves very basic bodily functions: eating and drinking.[14] We ingest with our mouths, we drink wine or juice (swallowing our saliva right along), we eat bread that will be digested and in part eventually expelled from our bodies. We do this eating and drinking in community. We may even share a common cup, our lips touching where other lips have been. The very practice that Jesus initiated in the upper room with his disciples before his impending death involves the embrace of the very stuff of life that fuels our bodies and that animates our spirits. To be fully alive is to be fully in the body—with all the beautiful and "disgusting" elements that involves.

Putting the psychology of disgust into the context of theological reflection on the birth of Jesus crystalizes an important insight: The squeamishness about biological realities was not only due to patriarchy with its male stigmatizing of female biology (though that was clearly a factor, too). The psychology of disgust likely shaped these theologians' aversion to a bloody and painful birth. But theologians should know that blood, saliva, or even meconium are innate to the human experience. A genuine theology of incarnation implies the birth of Jesus included these bodily elements.

The disgust impulse surely contributed to the spiritualizing and sanitizing of physical birth and of female biology. But much of this sanitizing can be chalked up to the consequences of living in a different time and place. From the perspective of our modern age, we can look back and criticize the reluctance or even derogation with which many of these theologians viewed the biological realities of childbirth. And we would be right to point out the obvious fact that these theologians were men and, as far as I can tell, they didn't consult women.

By understanding the important role Mary played, along with Jesus, in the story of salvation, we can gain empathy for these theologians. Mary was the "second Eve," a parallel to Jesus in the story of salvation: Just as Jesus set straight the sins of Adam, thereby making salvation from sin possible, so Mary rectified the sins of Eve, making it possible for humanity to follow in the way of holiness and purity in the life of the church. Both Mary and Jesus subverted the powers of sin and experienced its brokenness to provide a pathway for humanity to salvation—each in their own ways: Jesus as the savior and Mary as the blessed mother of Christ. But unfortunately, those profound insights were eclipsed by the gnostic and docetic instinct to cover over the icky, sticky, stinky body of Jesus.

THE BODY AND THE BLOOD

Then he took a loaf of bread, and when he had given thanks, he broke it and gave it to them, saying, "This is my body, which is given for you. Do this in remembrance of me." And he did the same with the cup after supper, saying, "This cup that is poured out for you is the new covenant in my blood." (Luke 22:19)

My body. Broken for you.

My blood. Poured out for you.

I've loved those words for a long time, ever since I began to understand what the Lord's Supper, or *Eucharist*, means—that the Son of God entered history and became flesh and blood. He suffered and died so that we might have life. The image of Jesus Christ distributing the bread and passing the wine to his disciples on the night he was betrayed, before undergoing a brutal death on the cross, both haunts me and gives me hope. His blood was shed, and somehow in the shedding of that blood and in the breaking of that body, new life springs forth.

In the Bible, there's power in blood. But that power was often misunderstood, and even feared. In the ancient Hebrew purity (Levitical) codes, female menstruation was considered unclean: "When a woman has a discharge of blood that is her regular discharge from her body, she shall be in her impurity for seven days, and whoever touches her shall be unclean until the evening" (Leviticus 15:19). The code goes on to clarify that even what she touches, or sits on, or wears, during her menstruation period is unclean; those who touch her suffer the same fate. After seven days following the end of her menstrual period, she is clean again. But if her menstruation is unusually long or if an emission of blood occurs at an irregular time, a ritual sacrifice by the priest was required for her purification. The priestly code offered pathways for purification in tandem with the cycles of female biology. Cleansing the impurities caused by blood required the expulsion of yet more blood—of animals.

The Old Testament isn't just concerned with female bodily impurities. Male bodily functions were sources of uncleanliness and impurity, too. In the Levitical code, a "discharge from his member" would result in the declaration that he was ritually unclean (Leviticus 15:2–15). The text is unclear as to what a discharge is, but it was likely infection in the penis that led to an emission of blood or pus (possibly gonorrhea). Just like the ritually impure woman, anything the unclean man touched, sat upon, or wore (or anyone who touched him) required washing with water for purification and required a priestly sacrifice of pigeons or turtledoves for purification (Leviticus 15:14). Semen from ejaculation was also considered a source of ritual uncleanliness that required purification (Leviticus 15:16–18). The discharge, whether in masturbation or sexual union, required bathing and washing of affected clothes. Sexuality, blood, and the emissions of the body were mysterious realities to be carefully monitored and attended to within the life of a community. Furthermore, sex was confined to the privacy of the home, rather than openly practiced—as was common in pagan temple worship. Much of the concern about bodily functions was based in a fundamental, though unmistakably primitive concern, not just for spiritual purity but also for health and well-being.

The three synoptic Gospels each includes a story about Jesus healing a woman from an unceasing "flow of blood" (Matthew 9:20–22; Mark 5:24–34; Luke 8:43–48). The texts are somewhat ambiguous about what the flow or "issue" of blood is, but it likely refers to a continued, uncontrollable menstruation, as referenced in the Levitical code. Whatever the precise diagnosis, the woman was considered ritually unclean by Jewish law and, while she may not have experienced isolation because of her condition, she was forbidden from going to the temple because of her impurity.[15]

In healing her, Jesus brings to her a greater salvation than the temple could offer. Jesus, a faithful
Jew and a rabbi to boot, didn't show contempt for
Hebraic ceremonial codes or make light of them. But
his acts of healing, which often involved physically
touching the ritually unclean, impure, and even dis-
eased, revealed his compassion in the context of the
messy, icky, sticky, stinky human experience. He tra-
versed boundaries of disgust to touch and heal
bodies.

The Bible includes more than concerns about
bodily functions and their impurities. Elsewhere
in the Bible, bodily fluids represent healing and
symbolize new life. Animal blood was necessary for
ritual purification. Jesus's death on the cross, with
water and blood spilling out of his side, represents
the ultimate picture of life coming through
death—through the broken, opened elements of the
body. And prior to Jesus's death, the meal of anticipation, remembrance, and fellowship with his disciples included wine that represented "my blood of
the covenant which is poured out for many for the
forgiveness of sins" (Mark 14:24).

The blood of Jesus. The body of Jesus. The birth
of Jesus through the body of Mary, with all the blood
that comes with real and beautiful human birth.

The eternal, divine Son of God fully entered our

human experience. The humanity of Jesus means there wasn't a painless, completely silent night. If the Son of God assumed true humanity by being born of Mary, his birth was a physical and bloody one. And Mary no doubt felt it.

But a challenge confronts us. Why should the logic of the incarnation apply to the birth (the delivery) of Jesus, but not to his conception in the womb of Mary? A question we must consider in the next step of our journey is whether the *in-carnation* implies a fully human procreative process. Which is to say, intercourse.

This question didn't occur to early theologians because their assumptions about biology differed from ours. In their understanding, the sexual organs and menstrual blood of the mother contained all the substance needed for the procreation of a child. The father, by injecting his semen (which back then they considered a form of blood) into the body of the mother, provided the "heat," the generative principle, necessary for the creation of a life. The male semen activated generation of new life upon contact with the female menstrual blood. But everything needed materially for life was there, inside the woman's body.[16] Crucially, the mother also provided the womb, a space for incubation, for that life to develop.

Within the ancient biological framework of the virgin birth, the Holy Spirit provided the spark necessary to activate the human construction material already present in Mary, giving rise to the virginally conceived embryo, Jesus Christ. While it was still considered a miracle, because God rather than a human male provided the generative heat necessary for procreation, the idea of a virginal conception raised no biological contradictions in those days.[17] Miracle? Yes. Biological contradiction? No.

In the early church, theologians accepted the virginal conception as the mechanism for the incarnation. In their eyes, this miracle gave proof that God really became a human being in and through Mary's body. They saw no biological or theological inconsistencies with a virginal conception. It wouldn't have occurred to them—or to the authors of Matthew and Luke—that the logic of incarnation might call for something different: a conception through sexual intercourse between a woman and a man.

But let's fast-forward to today. Seen through the lens of a contemporary biological understanding of procreation, the notion of a virginal conception appears to conflict with its original intention— which was to affirm the reality of the incarnation. Let's state the problem directly: The incarnation means that the Son of God became a true human being. But can a true human being come from a virginal conception?

Most of us will readily affirm that Jesus was birthed in a fully human way: a beautiful and bloody birth. But now we must consider whether to take that one step further—not just a normal human birth, but a fully human conception as the beginning of the incarnation of the divine Son of God.

Before answering that question, we have further to go on our journey. We need to talk about sex.

NOTES

1. Ambrose, *Letter 42*, in *Saint Ambrose: Letters*, translated by Sister Mary Melchior Beyenka in *The Fathers of the Church: A New Translation*, vol. 26 (New York: Fathers of the Church, Inc., 1954), 227.

2. Ambrose, *Letter LXIII*, in Philip Schaff et al., eds., *The Nicene and Post-Nicene Fathers*, 1st series: 14 vols.; 2nd series: 13 vols. (Buffalo, NY: Christian Literature, 1886–98: Reprint Peabody, MA: Hendrickson, 1996), vol. 10, 461.

3. J. N. D. Kelly, *Early Christian Doctrines*, revised edition (New York: HarperOne, 1978), 497.

4. Augustine, *Sermons* 191, in *Saint Augustine: Sermons on the Liturgical Seasons*, translated by Sister Mary Sarah Muldowney (New York: Fathers of the Church, Inc., 1959), 29, in *The Fathers of the Church: A New Translation*, vol. 38 (New York: Fathers of the Church, Inc., 1954).

5. Kelly, *Early Christian Doctrines*, 493.

6. See the introduction to the apocryphal books in the *New Oxford Annotated Bible: New Revised Standard Version with the Apocrypha*, ed. Bruce M. Metzger and Roland E. Murphy (New York: Oxford University Press, 1994).

7. *New Oxford Annotated Bible: New Revised Standard Version with the Apocrypha.*

8. Kelly, *Early Christian Doctrines*, 492.

9. Ibid.

10. Ibid., 493.

11. Peter Brown, *The Body and Society: Men, Women, and Sexual Renunciation in Early Christianity* (New York: Columbia University Press, 1988: Reprint, 2008), 50. For an extensive discussion of Jerome's interaction with Helvidius and Jovinian, see David Hunter, "Helvidius, Jovinian, and the Virginity of Mary in Late Fourth-Century Rome," *Journal of Early Christian Studies* 1, no. 1 (1993): 47–71, 53. Also see Brown, *The Body and Society*, 366–86.

12. Excerpts from Theodotos LIX, 3. Cited in Paula

Fredricksen, *Sin: The Early History of an Idea* (Princeton: Princeton University Press, 2012), 69.

13. See Richard Beck's explanation of Paul Rozin's experiment in *Unclean: Meditations on Purity, Hospitality, and Mortality* (Eugene, OR: Wipf & Stock, 2011), 1–3.

14. Beck, *Unclean*, 111–14.

15. Amy-Jill Levine, "Discharging Responsibility: Matthean Jesus, Biblical Law, and Hemorrhaging Woman," in *Treasures New and Old: Recent Contributions to Matthean Studies*, ed. David R. Bauer and Mark Alan Powell (Atlanta: Society of Biblical Literature, 1996), 379–97, 388.

16. Andrew Lincoln, *Born of a Virgin? Reconceiving Jesus in the Bible, Tradition, and Theology* (Grand Rapids, MI: Eerdmans, 2013), 256.

17. Lincoln, *Born of a Virgin?*, 262.

2

WHAT'S SO BAD ABOUT GOOD SEX?

One of the earliest sleepovers I can remember was mildly traumatic. Late at night, my friend treated a group of us pre-teen boys to the R-rated film *Excalibur*. Granted, this movie is tame by most standards today—compared to *Game of Thrones*, it might as well be an after-school special—but it was the first time I'd seen violence, nudity, and sex like that. For me, a Southern Baptist pastor's kid, John Boorman's portrayal of the legend of King Arthur and the Knights of the Round Table brought me into a whole new world of sensuality. At once mysterious and repulsive, it nearly made me physically sick.

Watching *Excalibur* made me feel like I had

opened a door into a world governed by dark spirits and populated by scantily clad, writhing flesh. My youthful guilt ruined the entire sleepover for me. I was so upset, my parents came and got me in the middle of the night. My conscience was far more innocent back then, but in retrospect, I doubt the guilt I experienced was the conviction of the Holy Spirit; it was more likely the result of encountering the unknown for the first time—and apparently too soon.

While my parents weren't overly legalistic, sex was rarely discussed in our family, and television viewing was closely monitored. Sexuality was shrouded in mystery and tinged with prohibition. As a parent of two young children, I can appreciate the vigilance. My five-year-old is disturbingly proficient at navigating On Demand and looking up YouTube videos on the iPad, and it's hard enough to keep him from a too-violent episode of *Teenage Mutant Ninja Turtles.* I can't imagine the challenges we'll face when he launches into puberty.

When I entered my early teen years I, like countless other teenagers venturing into that delightfully exotic post-puberty world, discovered the allure of sensual and sexual images. The most reliable source for those images was MTV. The channel was off limits by house-rules, but that didn't keep me from the occasional viewing. One early evening, while chan-nel-surfing, I discovered Madonna's "Like a Virgin" video. The "virgin," writhing on stage in a white wedding gown, transformed the image of the pure, patiently waiting bride-to-be into a powerful sexual icon, a symbol of sensual power and sexual freedom. Madonna stole the virgin concept and gave it a new meaning—and the fact that her name is also a com-mon title for Jesus's mother added a religious subtext to her sensuality. I wasn't thinking about any of this at the time, but it's clear that more was going on with Madonna's transformation of that image than I could have understood back then.

My mom woke me from my adolescent trance with the unwelcome message that dinner was ready. For countless teenagers like me, the pop icon became a momentary object of youthful desire. But Madonna was directly tapping into—subverting, even—the paradox of the male fascination with vir-ginity as simultaneously something to be revered, something to be desired, and something to be con-quered. Female virginity has long been subjected to the patriarchal confluence of desire and objectifica-tion, and she was troubling the waters of all those.

The Strange Doctrine of the Perpetual Virginity of Mary

Christianity's historic admiration of Mary puts the male fascination with female virginity on center stage. The church designated her as the paragon of virtue; her virginity and motherhood collide in a paradox. Some theologians took her virginity all the way (so to speak). They insisted on Mary's lifelong virginity; this meant her marriage to Joseph was an unusual arrangement—a Platonic relationship. Perhaps they had separate beds! In the minds of many theologians, Mary became a paragon of chastity and a forever-holy, sexually abstinent mother of both Jesus and the church.

Origen (185–254 CE), best known today for his controversial view of universal salvation, was the first theologian to explicitly endorse Mary's "perpetual virginity." He believed that Mary's womb physically opened in the birth of Jesus, but he also taught that Mary remained sexually chaste—she was a lifelong virgin. Just as Jesus served as the model of sexual purity for men, so Mary became the model of chastity for women; both were, in Origen's view, lifelong virgins.[1]

But to affirm this about Mary, Origen had to solve a problem: The Gospels mention Jesus's siblings (Matthew 13:55; Mark 6:3). So how did they get there, Origen? He proposed they were Jesus's *half* siblings, brothers and sisters from another mother—Joseph's former wife, who was deceased. The basis for this solution comes from the *Gospel of James*, which presents Joseph as a significantly older widower when he was engaged to Mary. Joseph had children from his earlier marriage who then became Jesus's step-siblings. Jerome offered another version of this solution, arguing that "brothers" could be interpreted as "cousins." But a little Greek study rules that out, since the designated Greek word for cousin (*anemisios*) wasn't used in the problematic verses.[2]

The Bible doesn't reference Mary's perpetual virginity. But in the hands of creative and resolute readers, the Bible can be read to support nearly any position. And in those days, "literal" (plain or commonsense) interpretations constituted only one option among several. The more interesting approaches dug past the surface-level of the text, searching for a deeper spiritual, theological, or moral meaning. The words served like a code for something more significant—allegories of a higher truth. Such allegorical interpretations also sought to derive meaning from unclear or controversial texts. The Song of Solomon, filled with highly charged erotic references, became a prime candidate for such readings in the early church and into the medieval period. The surface-level references to erotic love between a man and a woman were commonly interpreted as an allegory of Christ's spiritual love for the church, his bride.

The theologian Ambrose applied such an allegorical reading to the Song of Solomon. He zeroed in on an obscure passage in that book: "A garden enclosed is my sister, my spouse; a spring shut up, a fountain sealed" (Song of Solomon 4:12). Ambrose read the "enclosed" garden (some contemporary translations read "locked up") as legitimating the vocation of religious chastity and as confirming Mary's perpetual virginity. But he also read the passage as a message from Christ to the church, "which he desires to be a virgin, without spot, without a wrinkle" and "everywhere shut in by the wall of chastity."[3]

If Ambrose had made these claims in a seminary paper today, his biblical studies professor might charge him with *eisegesis* because he inputs meaning *into* the text, rather than interpreting the meaning in its original context. But to Ambrose, it didn't matter that the author of the Song of Solomon didn't know about Mary—or Jesus, for that matter. The images and the references to virgin brides foreshadowed and legitimated the doctrine of Mary's perpetual virginity. But it also served to justify Ambrose's affirmation of lifelong sexual abstinence as a religious vocation.

All well-known Christian theologians within the earliest years of Christianity accepted the virginal conception as the mechanism for the entrance of Jesus into the world. But not everyone joined the chorus of praise for lifelong chastity. There are good reasons to oppose the idea of the perpetual virginity of Mary.

For one thing, Matthew's Gospel appears to directly contradict the notion: "When Joseph awoke from sleep, he did as the angel of the Lord commanded him; he took her as his wife, but had no marital relations with her until she had borne a son; and he named him Jesus" (Matthew 1:24–25). The word "until" implies that the couple consummated their marriage sometime after Jesus's birth—in other words, they didn't have sex *before* the birth, but they sure did afterward. Subsequent references to Jesus's siblings in Matthew support that interpretation.

By and large, though, the doctrine of the perpetual virginity of Mary won the day, becoming the dominant view throughout much of Christianity. Catholic, Eastern Orthodox, and some Protestant traditions still officially revere her as "Mary, Ever

Virgin." And Joseph is therefore portrayed as an older man—old enough to have had a wife and kids before Mary and Jesus. Don't believe me? Go look at a crèche!

PURITY BALLS AND CONSERVATIVE CHRISTIAN CULTURE

I grew up in a conservative evangelical environment, so I'm no stranger to purity covenants and abstinence commitments. My youth pastors were more restrained than some, so I never experienced some of its more outlandish varieties. While I heard many talks about the importance of abstinence before marriage, and even delivered a few myself as a well-meaning youth minister, I'd never heard of anything like "Purity Balls."

These unusual ceremonies, unique to fundamentalist Christian culture, promote sexual purity and abstinence for young girls. In one variation, fathers bring their twelve-year-old daughters to a ballroom dance, dressed in white wedding-like gowns, with the intention of formalizing their commitment to abstinence before marriage. The events typically culminate in a covenanting ritual; the daughters kneel before a wooden cross and pledge their virginity to Jesus and, apparently, to their fathers, too.

Some websites extol the glory of Purity Balls, sharing photographs of the events for the disbelievers: Fathers holding their daughters in a solemn, protective embrace; young girls in white dresses laying bouquets at the foot of a tall wooden cross on the middle of a gymnasium/dance floor. As a father of a young daughter, I find it creepy. Worst of all, it reinforces the patriarchal notion that men have control over their daughters' bodies and that female virginity is to be protected at all costs, like a valuable commodity—but one owned by men.

A message comes across loud and clear to young people: If you "lose your virginity," you will be forever marred and stained. A heavy burden to bear, indeed. One website dedicated to providing resources for Purity Balls suggests that the father should take responsibility for ensuring that his daughter remains true to her vow of sexual purity. I suspect they greet their daughters' prom dates with a shotgun in hand. Ultimately, though, the grave task of preserving the commodity of virginity is laid at the feet of the girls themselves. Boys might be asked to sign abstinence pledges, but there are no purity balls for them. This reinforces the double standard of the male as the natural sexual aggressor and of the female, in the absence of their gun-toting fathers, as solely responsible for fending them off.

Purity balls and other ritualized abstinence commitments reflect an anxiety within fundamentalist Christianity. Surrounded by an increasingly secular culture, with ever-evolving access points to "the world" thanks to technology and social media, teenagers are subject to innumerable sexual temptations. While there's surely truth to this, the valuing of sexual purity as central to Christian discipleship intensifies this anxiety and detracts from, as Jesus puts it, "weightier matters of the law: justice and mercy and faith" (Matthew 23:23).

The focus on individual, and primarily *female*, sexual morality sidelines other concerns. It's crazy to realize how much justice and righteousness, peacemaking, care for the environment, solidarity with the marginalized and oppressed, and even loving your neighbor, pale in comparison to sexual morality in so many of our churches. As we've seen, this goes back to the earliest days of the church, a day in which virginity was prized as a valued symbol of religious dedication and of Christian faithfulness. In those days, an extensive debate took place about whether celibacy ("consecrated virginity") was holier than marriage.

RESISTING THE CULT OF VIRGINITY

Ambrose and Jerome advocated a rigorous Christianity, one that valued sexual purity above married sex.[4] They argued that the perpetual virginity of Mary proved the superiority of celibacy. But a few plucky theologians insisted on the equality of marriage to singleness. Jovinian believed that marriage and celibacy ought to be equally prized within the Christian life. Mary should be revered both for her chastity prior to her marriage, and for her faithfulness to Joseph throughout it. And Helvidius taught that following the birth of Jesus, Mary and Joseph experienced a typical marriage, including sexuality and procreation. He insisted that no one should have to blush at the thought of Mary having intercourse with her husband.[5]

So much squabbling about Mary's virginity! But all these guys agreed on one thing: her sexual purity undergirded her role in God's salvation. Throughout much of Christian history, virginity has often been prized as the primary pathway to holiness and evidence of discipline and faithfulness to God. This assumption met with vigorous objections during the Protestant Reformation, when Martin Luther and John Calvin urged priests and other Christians to find a marriage partner and get it on (to paraphrase them). In a letter to a lawyer, Luther offers some pastoral advice: "Kiss and rekiss your wife. Let her love and be loved." And then he concludes his admonition: "A married life is a paradise, even where all else is wanting."[6]

The Catholics responded to these marriage-loving Protestants by doubling-down on their stance on the priority of sexual chastity over married sexuality, stating in no uncertain terms at the Council of Trent: "Virginity and celibacy are better and more blessed than the bond of matrimony!"[7] And lest they be misunderstood, the Council warned that anyone who doesn't affirm the superiority of celibacy to marriage stands outside of the church and of salvation—Anathema!

For all their enthusiasm about marriage and sexuality, even Luther and Calvin affirmed the perpetual virginity of Mary. Nonetheless, in the Protestant churches marriage overtook the place of chaste singleness as the ideal for the Christian life. For most Christians today, erotic love between monogamous, covenanted partners seems natural, right, and holy. Indeed, the tide may have turned: Singleness plays second fiddle to marriage in much of Christian culture. While the value of living one's Christian life as a single person should never be undermined, I side with those who affirm the equal value of marriage and singleness in the Christian life. No blushing needed.

To be fair, the sexual purity initiatives in Christianity also affirm the gift of sexuality within marriage. But the intensity with which many conservatives focus on sexual morality above social justice concerns, for example, reveals a problematic imbalance. To some degree, the problem goes all the way back to the early church's linkage of sin with sex. Jerome illustrates this problem when he proclaims that, "In view of the purity of the body of Christ, all sexual intercourse is unclean."[8]

The notion of Mary's perpetual virginity offered a way for these early church writers to emphasize Mary as a model of sexual chastity. For many today, it's unbecoming or even offensive that male theologians decree this role for Mary—a role she never claimed for herself. The title "Mary, Ever Virgin" puts virginity on a pedestal, and implies an association of sexuality with sin. For the source of this, we need look no further than the great theologian, Augustine of Hippo.

Immaculate Semen: Sex and Sin under the Influence of Augustine

In grade school, I got into a heated debate with some friends about whether my parents had ever had sex. I lost the debate, but I won an important prize: an education that sex is how babies are made. I had insisted that my parents didn't have sex and never would have had sex, because they were Christians (and my dad was a pastor!). In their defense, my parents didn't teach me this. Christian culture did, through its secretive and negative attitudes toward sex. My friends corrected my mistaken belief—my sister and I didn't drop out of the sky from the beak of a stork.

The association of sin with sex comes from a long history in Christian theology, and the two were forever linked through the doctrine of *original sin*. For this, we can mostly thank Augustine, along with Ambrose, his pastor. Augustine taught that original sin resulted from the disobedience of our forefather and foremother, Adam and Eve. When they ate fruit from the forbidden tree, they were transformed from perfect creatures with rightly ordered passions, to severely flawed creatures with disordered desires.

Due to "the Fall" of Adam and Eve, the lusts of the flesh are uncontrollable apart from God's intervening grace. Even after grace intervenes, human beings suffer the morally debilitating effects of original sin, until they receive resurrected bodies.

This act of disobedience resulted in severe consequences for all subsequent humans (you and me included) because all humanity exists *in* Adam and Eve. The "stuff" of which our spiritual natures (our souls) are made is passed along via procreation, beginning with our fallen fore-parents. For Augustine, original sin spreads like a virus of the soul. The host of the virus? The semen. Thus, sin is passed along *seminally*—through the sexual act. Because of the sin of Adam and Eve, each of us is severely damaged from the moment of our conception. And God considers us guilty for their sins.

In other words, we're all screwed from the start—except for Jesus.

You might protest: That's not fair! And you would be right.

Nonetheless, Augustine's influence on Christianity's understanding of sin reaches far and wide. Many Christians feel an urgency about baptizing their infants, because they believe it removes the guilt of original sin. If their baby were to die unexpectedly and tragically, at least they'd be covered by God's forgiveness through baptism.

Here's where the virgin birth comes in.

With Augustine, the virgin birth acquired even greater significance in Christianity. The virginal conception allowed Jesus to escape the fate that is unavoidable for the rest of us. The supernatural conception of Jesus by the Holy Spirit disrupted the flow of sin into humanity; it removed the mechanism (sex) and the medium (human semen) that distributes original sin. Augustine's pastor, Ambrose, reasoned that the virgin birth protected baby Jesus from even an *association* with sinful sex. The virginal conception allowed Jesus to be born with "a stainless body" unpolluted by sin and by "any admixture of defilement."[9] God through the Holy Spirit provided the seed that activated the generation of life and bypassed the role of the human male. The Holy Spirit conceived Jesus in Mary through "immaculate semen."[10]

There's another phrase they never taught me in seminary!

No man, no sex, no human semen, and no sin of Adam and Eve. Jesus was born free from original sin *and* the guilt that came with it, so Jesus could live a sinless life. And he could save his people from their sins and wash away their—and our—guilt.

44

Augustine still had to confront the vexing problem that Mary was a sinner, too. Ultimately, this problem led to the suggestion by later theologians that *Mary herself* was immaculately conceived: God removed the stain of original sin from Mary at her conception by a miraculous act of the Spirit in the womb of her mother, whom tradition has named Anna.

Augustine was brilliant, but he was also wrong at times. His theory of original sin was based on a faulty Latin translation of the original Greek text of Romans 5:12. This translation led Augustine to interpret Paul as saying that all human nature is included in the sins of Adam and Eve, and therefore *all humans* are automatically and equally guilty of the sins of our primeval pair. The correct translation of the relevant passage in Romans reads, "death spread to all *because* all have sinned" (not *in whom* all have sinned—the translation Augustine read).[11] Had Augustine been reading the accurate translation, he may have come to a very different conclusion: you and I are responsible for our own sin—not for the sins of Adam and Eve.

SIN AFTER THE FALL

We can respect Augustine's brilliance, but let's be honest: his view of the transmission of sin and guilt is problematic. It's based on outdated biological assumptions, for one thing. It's grounded in a faulty translation of the Bible, for another. And finally, it's just theologically problematic that the guilt of the first humans ("Adam and Eve") would be automatically applied to the rest of us, from the moment of our conception.

I recall holding and rocking our firstborn child, Ella, and thinking about Augustine's theory of original sin. How could my precious baby be considered guilty by God for sins she hadn't yet committed—blamed for the deeds of others? If God is love, surely God's love for my daughter is infinitely deeper and richer than even my own love for my beautiful, innocent baby.

Don't get me wrong: I believe sin is real, and I affirm that we're all sinners. I resonate with Reinhold Niebuhr, the theologian who suggested that original sin is the only Christian doctrine proven by empirical evidence. Just turn on the news if you want proof of our propensity to sin. I affirm that sin is a real, pervasive, and unavoidable aspect of the human condition. But our understanding of sin must move beyond Augustine's theory of a Fall. Sin is the name for that perverted aspect of the human condition in which, through willful actions, we disrupt our relationships—horizontally with others and vertically with God.

Sin isn't the *lack* of moral and spiritual freedom, but our deliberate misuse of it.[12] By misusing our capacity to make choices, we negatively affect our relationships—with God, with each other, and with creation. Our sin affects a complex matrix of structures, systems, and influences. In this sense, we do distribute and inherit sin throughout the generations. And we can certainly constrain our freedom by continually making wrong choices—that's how addictions often work, for example. We learn how to sin from everyone around us—and from the societies and cultures that shape us. And yes, we inherit dispositions and limitations that render us ready-made to become sinners in our own right. Just give us time—we'll get there! But please don't blame me for the sins of some ancient couple in a primordial garden. I've got enough to atone for all on my own.

Unfortunately, Augustine's theology of sin went viral: it's greatly influenced much of Christianity. And the virgin birth stories came to mean something very foreign to Matthew and Luke. After Augustine, the virgin birth serves as the great

47

end-around, eluding the effects of original sin and disrupting its cycle. The Virgin Mary became ever more deeply fixed in the Christian imagination as the paragon of virtue and chastity. Just as her son Jesus bypassed sex in every way, she foregoes sexuality in favor of a life fully dedicated to God and Christ.

At the root of this high-minded, well-meaning theology lies a deeply embedded assumption about the intertwining of sin, sex, and procreation. But the vigilant attempts to shield Jesus's birth from any hint of human sexuality ended up undermining rather than affirming the incarnation, the *in-fleshing* of God. If creation is good, and if human sexuality is a part of that creation, then there's no obvious reason why the Son of God had to evade it. If divinity can fit into created human reality; there's no apparent reason why human procreation should be deemed unworthy as the mechanism of Jesus's conception.

We're still far from the conclusion of our journey. But at this point, we can at least affirm that the logic of the incarnation implies that sexual intercourse *could* be a perfectly adequate means through which the Son of God became a true, human being.

We can appreciate the reasons for the traditions that underlie the doctrine of the virgin birth while also thinking critically about them. We should notice that so much of Christian theology about the virgin birth and the virginity of Mary resulted from very imaginative and culturally influenced men. For much of male-dominated Christianity, Mary's virginity became the most important thing about her.

But Mary seems comparatively uninterested in her virginal status. Her only reference to her virginity is an exclamation of disbelief that God would do such a thing through her: "How can this be, since I am a virgin?" (Luke 1:34).

MARY'S FREEDOM SONG OR, WHEN GOD TURNS THE WORLD UPSIDE DOWN

We don't know much for certain about Mary. But we know she was a young Jewish girl between twelve and sixteen (marriageable age for women in the first century) when she gave birth to Jesus. Presumably, Mary had only recently arrived at that marriageable age when she was pregnant with Jesus, her first child. She was probably poor, too. The sacrifice Joseph and Mary presented at the temple for the dedication of Jesus suggests their low socio-economic status. Poor people could substitute turtle-doves and pigeons for a lamb (Luke 2:22–24). Another hint of Mary and Joseph's low social status comes in Matthew: When Herod decrees to kill the firstborn in Bethlehem, their lack of power as Jews living under Roman rule forces them to migrate to Egypt.

I used to think of Mary as a twenty- or even thirty-something woman who had patiently and faithfully waited, sacrificially holding out her purity for God. I pictured her as a mostly self-sufficient woman, with choices, options, and resources at her disposal. But the Gospels paint a different picture. Mary's "Song of Praise" in Luke, known as the *Magnificat*, is her poetic and prophetic response to the angel's surprising announcement that she would give birth to the long-awaited Messiah of Israel. A few highlights:

> My soul magnifies the Lord,
> and my spirit rejoices in God my Savior,
> for he has looked with favor on the lowliness of his servant.
> Surely, from now on all generations will call me blessed,
> for the Mighty One has done great things for me,
> and holy is his name. (Luke 1:46–49)

And then:

He has brought down the powerful from their
  thrones,
and lifted up the lowly;
he has filled the hungry with good things,
and sent the rich away empty. (Luke 1:52–53)

As an economically poor, socially vulnerable, Jewish girl living under Roman occupation, Mary understood and felt the cries of her people for liberation. She's joyously shocked to be pronounced the mother of the Messiah.[13] But the phrase "lowliness of his servant" doesn't just refer to Mary's personal social situation; rather, the song represented Israel in the context of oppression and subjection in the often-hostile Roman Empire.[14] Luke, through Mary's song, gives voice to the expected liberation of Israel from its oppressive political rulers. Luke understood Jesus as the Messiah who had come to bring salvation to his people; a salvation that gave new life and hope in the context of oppression. In other words, Jesus in Luke (and in Matthew) is both savior and liberator.

The Magnificat doesn't indicate that God chose Mary because of her sexual purity or chastity. Rather, Mary expresses wonder that God turns things upside down. God favors the lowly of society, and in so doing subverts the typical ways of the world. God gives hope to the hopeless and dignity to marginalized persons.

Through both Luke and Matthew, God elevates the vulnerable, the oppressed, and the outsider. God's heart for the "lowly" hits us square in the face in the Beatitudes, the most famous verses from the Gospels. These powerful teachings of Jesus express God's heart for the poor and God's warning to the rich who ignore and perpetuate injustice:

Blessed are you who are poor,
  for yours is the kingdom of God.
Blessed are you who are hungry now,
  for you will be filled.
Blessed are you who weep now,
  for you will laugh. (Luke 6:20–21)

Attention to the socio-economic context of Mary changes the direction of our how we think of Mary. The issue of her virginity fades from view.

In the Gospels' narration of God's salvation, the virginal conception plays an important role. It shows that God does a new thing through the person of Jesus Christ. But otherwise, the virginal conception and the virginity of Mary should not command our attention. The focal point shifts instead to God changing the course of history, fulfilling God's promise to Israel of a Messiah and expanding that promise to include a salvation for the entire world. God has become flesh, God has become Emmanuel, "God-with-us." Mary's vulnerable and marginalized status powerfully illustrates God's upending of history and reversal of expected fortunes.

Christian theologians insisted that God brings salvation into the world through incarnation. The two Gospels, with their stories of the divine conception by the Spirit, highlight this salvation by establishing the unique origins of the Son of God. They are not encomiums of Mary's chastity or lifelong sexual purity. The logic of incarnation proclaims that God enters the frailty, brokenness, and bodily beauty of the world and becomes a part of it. He takes it on, all of it, and in so doing proclaims it as *good*, though in need of salvation. God heals, redeems, and liberates in and through Jesus.

Our journey into the question of the virgin birth is starting to take an unexpected shape. At this stage, we've discovered a new slant on the manger scene.

For many Christians, it's difficult to seriously consider the possibility that Jesus Christ was born of a normal, biological procreative process. The weight of Christianity's traditions heavily tips the scales toward affirmation of a miraculous, virginal conception. And we now understand why.

The links of virginity with holiness, on the one hand, and sexuality with sin on the other hand, shape our perceptions of Mary and of Jesus's birth. For many early theologians, sex and sin were deeply intertwined; thus, they couldn't even fathom the possibility that Jesus might have been conceived through human intercourse. For those of us who are deeply influenced by this tradition, it's difficult to envision a different manger scene: one in which Jesus was born of a woman *and* of a man.

Christianity has inscribed in our imaginations a picture of a virginal conception, a young Jewish girl submitting to the "Annunciation," a surprised but honorable (and elderly!) Joseph, and a magical silent night. It's difficult to imagine alternative scenarios that diverge from that sacred story: a normal human conception that led to the birth of a fully human Jesus. But what's "normal," these days, about conception?

NOTES

1. J. N. D. Kelly, *Early Christian Doctrines*, revised edition (New York: HarperOne, 1978), 493.

2. C. S. Mann, *Mark* (Garden City, NY: Doubleday, 1986),

258. See also Tim Perry and Daniel Kendall, SJ, *The Blessed Virgin Mary* (Grand Rapids, MI: Eerdmans, 2013), 11–13.

3. Ambrose, *Letter LXIII*, in Philip Schaff et al., eds., *The Nicene and Post-Nicene Fathers*, 1st series: 14 vols.; 2nd series: 13 vols. (Buffalo, NY: Christian Literature, 1886–98: Reprint Peabody, MA: Hendrickson, 1996), vol. 10, 461.

4. See the discussion in David Hunter, "Helvidius, Jovinian, and the Virginity of Mary in Late Fourth-Century Rome," *Journal of Early Christian Studies* 1, no. 1 (1993): 47–71, and Peter Brown, *The Body and Society: Men, Women, and Sexual Renunciation in Early Christianity* (New York: Columbia University Press, 1988: Reprint, 2008), 366–86.

5. Hunter, "Helvidius, Jovinian, and the Virginity of Mary," 50.

6. Cited in James Reston, *Luther's Fortress: Martin Luther and His Reformation Under Siege* (New York: Basic Books, 2015), 87.

7. Council of Trent in Canon 10 of its 24th session.

8. Jerome, *Against Jovinianus* in *The Nicene and Post-Nicene Fathers*, 2nd series: 14 vols.; 2nd series: 13 vols. (Buffalo, NY: Christian Literature, 1886–98: Reprint Peabody, MA: Hendrickson, 1999), vol. 6, 1.20, 361.

9. Ambrose, *Concerning Repentance*, in Schaff et al., eds., *The Nicene and Post-Nicene Fathers*, vol. 10, 1.3.13, 331.

10. Ambrose, *Exposition on Luke* 2.56. See David Hunter, "Helvidius, Jovinian, and the Virginity of Mary," 58.

11. Tatha Wiley, *Original Sin: Origins, Developments, Contemporary Meanings* (Mahwah, NJ: Paulist, 2002), 61.

12. Also see Patricia Williams, *Doing without Adam and Eve: Sociobiology and Original Sin* (Minneapolis: Fortress Press, 2001), 45–47.

13. See Traci C. West, *Disruptive Christian Ethics: When Racism and Women's Lives Matter* (Louisville: Westminster John Knox, 2006), 71–111, for a discussion of the application of Mary's Magnificat to economic and political policies that affect women.

14. Richard Horsley, *The Liberation of Christmas: The Infancy Narratives in Social Context* (New York: Continuum, 1993).

3

VIRGIN BIRTHS HAPPEN TO SHARKS, BUT NOT TO HUMANS

Virgin births aren't as miraculous as you think.

Just ask Andrew Fields, a geneticist with Stony Brook University, and his team of researchers. They discovered occurrences of virgin births among a population of smalltooth sawfish, an endangered species of river-dwelling rays (appropriately named, with noses like double-sided saws).[1] While combing through a database of 190 sawfish tagged between 2004 and 2013, something jumped out at the researchers. The genetic composition of seven of the rays revealed that each of them had only one parent, bearing the imprint of a mother, but not a father. Some of these seven *parthenogens* (offspring of a single parent, conceived via asexual procreation) might still be maneuvering through the rivers of southwest Florida. Perhaps they're still poking around with their long jagged noses, swimming examples of the marvelous capacity for life to perpetuate, despite odds stacked against them.

The discovery didn't completely surprise Fields because virgin births (technically: *asexual* conceptions) are not unheard of in the animal kingdom. Scientists have documented cases among fruit flies, fire ants, and wasps, among other insect and invertebrate life. But asexual reproduction has also occurred among lizards, chickens, turkeys, sharks, and other marine animals, as Fields and his team discovered.

On December 14, 2001, a female hammerhead shark gave birth in an Omaha zoo.[2] This perplexed the zookeepers because the mother had lived in captivity for over three years *apart from any males.* Because her captivity began prior to sexual development, this was a bona fide virginal conception. Within hours after the birth of her virgin-born pup, a stingray in the same tank killed the newborn. So much for miracles.

Then, in 2008, at the Virginia Aquarium in Virginia Beach, scientists performing an autopsy on a blacktip shark named Tidbit found a twelve-inch-long fetus inside her. Tidbit had lived apart from male blacktip sharks her entire life.[3] DNA testing confirmed the surprising conclusion: her pup's genetic material was derived entirely from Tidbit. There was no father in sight, either in the aquarium or in the pup's genome. In both cases, the pregnancies were determined to be the results of *parthenogenesis*, in other words, asexual conceptions. Like the hammerhead shark and her pup, the story of Tidbit's virgin birth ended in tragedy, not miracle: Both Tidbit and her fetus died during the pregnancy.

Scientists have natural explanations for the phenomenon. In one common version of *parthenogenesis*, a female fertilizes her own egg when "material that's split off from an egg as it divides—called a polar body—fuses back with the egg."[4] That material plays the role that sperm does in normal procreation, by activating self-fertilization.

Incredible, isn't it? But a miracle? No.

The existence of a scientific explanation doesn't make it unremarkable. Parthenogenesis sounds miraculous to those of us who weren't biology majors, but biologists, zoologists, and others know better. Sexual intercourse hasn't always been the only or main method of procreation. It's certainly not the most ancient one. The first living organisms, our most primordial ancestors, didn't have sex, but they did generate offspring (and we thank them for it).

Parthenogenesis occurs in varied ways, whether in fruit flies, wasps, sharks, lizards, or turkeys. But commonly, something other than male sperm triggers activation of the female egg, resulting in new life. A female-only species of whiptail lizard mastered a mating ritual in which an aggressor female behaves in prototypically male fashion, initiating extensive contact with the passive female but without inseminating her.[5] Aggressive friction provokes the eggs to activate, initiating procreation. Other examples of asexual reproduction abound. Who needs a male, when another female will work just fine? Or, as in the case of an extraordinary group of turkeys and chickens in the early 1950s, when an intrusive virus will do the trick?[6]

IF THE VIRGIN BIRTH WAS A MIRACLE, WHAT'S THE POINT OF ALL THIS SCIENCE?

Asexual reproduction occurs surprisingly often in non-mammalian animals and insects. At first glance, this lends scientific support to the traditional view of a supernatural divine conception. If virgin births happen to sharks and turkeys, why not to Mary, the mother of the Son of God? The theologian Origen used this argument to defend the virgin birth against skeptics. He pointed to a then-known instance of female-only reproduction in vultures, arguing that if birds can muster up a virginal conception, surely God could accomplish that uncommon feat in Mary.[7]

On the face of it, this is a compelling argument. Many people scratch their heads at this crazy notion that Jesus was born of a virgin. Irrational! Unreasonable! Nonscientific! But most people who shake their heads at this "outdated," ancient story don't realize that virginal conceptions happen with surprising regularity. And they're scientifically verified.

But there's a problem with trying to normalize the virgin birth by appealing to asexual reproduction in the natural world. While parthenogenesis occurs in nonhuman animals, it's never been verified in humans or any other mammals, for that matter—and it's not for a lack of trying. Scientists have searched for evidence across mammalian species. They've even tried to initiate virgin births in the laboratory, but to no avail. There's something about humans that renders virginal conceptions impossible from a biological point of view—at least as far as we know.

Successful fertilization and procreation of human life requires the contribution of both male sperm and a female egg, genetic contributions from a female and a male. Furthermore, the generation of a male embryo by fertilization requires genetic input from a male parent. With no human male involved in the procreation of Jesus, he would have lacked the Y chromosome crucial for determining male sex. There's a fascinating exception to this biological rule: either Mary *or* Jesus could have been intersex, or in the older terminology, a *hermaphrodite*. In the former case, Mary could have carried the Y chromosome; in the latter, Jesus could have lacked one.[8]

For many Christians, this discussion of parthenogenesis misses the point. The infancy narratives make no appeal to marvels of science. Furthermore, faith in the possibility of the virgin birth doesn't require the support of scientific verification.

For countless believers, the infancy narratives—
which they take to be revelation from God, pure and
simple—lie beyond the purview of science, a point
strongly implied by the appearance of the angel in
the story. To date, science has neither verified nor
falsified the existence of angels. So, the virginal conception is a divine miracle pure and simple. It's an
interruption of nature by supernatural power; a
spark of singularity disrupting the usual patterns,
processes, and rules of biology. Appeals to natural
phenomena only detract from the miraculous nature
of the story and the common belief that God can do
whatever God wants. Laws of nature be damned.

DIVINE ARTIFICIAL INSEMINATION

When skeptics ask, "Where did Jesus get his Y chromosome—you know, the one necessary for him to
be a *male human?*" some believers answer simply and
directly: *God provided it.* They point out that Jesus
was no ordinary human being. Born of a woman,
yes. But also, born of God! So, Jesus's divine origin
and nature means we can throw natural law out the
window. In 1908, Charles Briggs warned those who
leaned on science to support their belief in the virgin
birth: "The church has never thought of any such
thing as parthenogenesis."[9] Briggs insisted the Son

of God could become incarnate in whatever way he wished, unencumbered by the laws of biology and physics. God doesn't depend on scientific, biological processes to pull off a feat like the incarnation.

Fair enough. I empathize with the argument that God is, well, God. It's reasonable to suppose that God isn't necessarily constrained by the laws of creation. The incarnation marks a pivotal moment in history when the Son of God enters the world. Perhaps we should expect God to interrupt nature and human biology—signaling the momentous occasion.

But let's be honest. Faith doesn't absolve us from the use of reason. And we've got some serious issues to consider at this point.

Even if we grant God's power to perform miracles, we're still faced with a question about genetics and with the human nature of Jesus. If we accept a supernatural, virginal conception, we need to explain how Jesus was a true, human being. Every human being in the world—and presumably in the history of the world—has a genetic composition that includes 50 percent genetic input from a female and 50 percent genetic input from a male. But the virgin birth of Jesus casts normalcy aside, because there was no male biological parent. If Mary provided the female half of Jesus's genes, then she directly influenced half of Jesus's biology, physiology, and appearance. Who—or what—influenced the other half?

A couple of options arise. First, God perhaps created and inserted sperm into Mary's fallopian tube, where it traveled to meet her ovum (reproductive cell), initiating fertilization. In a more PG version of this option, God might have input the necessary male genetic material, or genetic code, directly into Mary's ovum. In either case, it stands to reason that God had to determine the composition of the genetic contribution from the missing male side. But on what basis? Perhaps God replicated Joseph's DNA and inscribed it into Jesus's forming genome. This would have been a very circuitous answer to the dilemma of how the virgin-born Jesus could have descended from the lineage of David since Joseph—not Mary—came from David's line.

Both editions of this version—sperm injection or DNA input—imply that God designed and actualized a genetic composition for Jesus that wasn't naturally inherited through biological processes. Arthur Peacocke, both a theologian and a biologist, probed the odd consequences of this notion: "What genetic information was encoded in these miraculously created genes? Did God give him a set to make his characteristics (shape of nose, color of hair, blood group, etc.) mimic what Joseph would have provided had he been involved—or what?"[10]

I'm open-minded about the use of genetic technology for medical and scientific purposes (though it raises complex moral and pragmatic issues). But I must admit, it's odd to imagine God fiddling around in some heavenly genetics laboratory, designing the zygote that would become Jesus of Nazareth.

This discussion isn't just nerdy and eccentric (though there's plenty of that here to go around). It exposes some conceptual problems with the traditional view of the virgin birth. At the very least, it's difficult to see how people can insist on the necessity of belief in the virgin birth, since it involves such conceptual gymnastics.

There's a second possibility, though: Perhaps God didn't create supernatural sperm or design the genetics of Jesus. Instead, imagine that he created a human zygote from nothing, or *de novo*, without using any physical material from Mary (i.e., bypassing her ovum) and directly implanted the divinely created zygote Jesus into the welcoming womb of Mary. The ultimate *in vitro* fertilization! In this scenario, Mary truly functions as a surrogate mother for Jesus.

But two problems emerge with this option. First, a *de novo* creation of zygote Jesus means that God interrupts the human evolutionary line to bring about the incarnation. God starts over with Jesus, so that he can redeem humanity through a pure and perfect human. But here's the problem with that: It's difficult to see how Jesus truly becomes one of us if his physical body didn't contain any preexisting human material. A *de novo* Jesus would have bypassed the long, storied history of human evolution. It's worth considering whether a supernaturally conceived, virgin-born Jesus would have completely shared our human nature.[11] It seems impossible.

Our problems with the virginal conception are mounting up. A supernaturally conceived Jesus would have been disconnected biologically from the very human nature he intended to redeem. The early theologians intuited this problem, though they knew nothing about evolution. They insisted that Jesus "took flesh" from Mary's body.[12] They had no problem with God removing Joseph's contribution (semen), but they drew the line at Mary. If Mary contributed nothing of physical substance to the body of her son, then Jesus didn't participate in the very human nature he intended to save. That concern relates to one of the most famous lines from the early church, penned by Gregory Nazianzen (329–390 CE): "For that which He has not assumed He has not healed; but that which is united to His Godhead is also saved."[13] Put in contemporary language: Jesus became us in every way, so he could heal us in every way.

These theologians insisted that Jesus needed to physically take something from our humanity so he could fully redeem us: that's the significance of the incarnation. A *de novo* zygote, created from no pre-existing human material, undercuts the redemptive intention of the incarnation: he became it, so he could heal it.

But if we grant that a *de novo* zygote Jesus undermines the logic of the incarnation, we must consider another possibility. Perhaps the traditional view of the virgin birth collapses under that same logical weight. For Jesus to become a true human being, did he need to "take flesh" from a mother *and* from a father, too?

This leads us into the second problem with a *de novo* zygote Jesus: He would have had no biological parents or grandparents, and no ancestors at all. It's difficult to reconcile this consequence with Paul's proclamation that Jesus was the "offspring of Abraham" (Galatians 3:16) and that he was "descended of David according to the flesh" (Romans 1:3). A miraculous zygote Jesus also creates a problem for the genealogies of Matthew and Luke, since both genealogies connect Jesus to David through Joseph.

Presumably, Joseph would have passed along to Jesus his Davidic, royal lineage through natural procreation—via sexual intercourse.

For those who affirm a virgin birth, the only possible answer to the dilemma of how Jesus received his royal, Messianic credentials is legal adoption, a solution possibly implied in Matthew's infancy narrative. The census in Bethlehem suggests that Joseph legalizes (adopts) Jesus as his son, though that's reading between the lines of the biblical text. While adoption might address how Jesus inherited his Messianic credentials, it doesn't solve the greater problem now raised by the logic of incarnation: Was Jesus really one of us?

JESUS CHRIST IS BLOOD OF OUR BLOOD AND BONE OF OUR BONE

My brother-in-law, Dan, met his biological mother for the first time recently. A college friend of Dan's, a social worker in Colorado, had recently acquired access to the information because of new, relaxed restrictions on adoption records. She offered to research public records and, with Dan's blessing, headed to the courthouse. Within twenty-four hours she emailed Dan a photograph of his mother surrounded by some of her family members, and the accompanying explanation: "I'm pretty certain this is your mother. And your siblings, too."

Dan, in his early fifties, had enjoyed a happy and fulfilled life. He didn't have a burning desire to discover his biological family, but this unanticipated discovery was now staring him in the face. As he gazed at the picture of his mom, his sisters, and his brothers, it was stunning. He'd always been an only child. It was wild for him to realize he had siblings walking around in the world, sharing the same DNA, the same mother.

Dan's friend, the adoption sleuth, took it upon herself to contact one of Dan's siblings, drive to her house, knock on her door, and to let her know that she had a brother who was open to meeting the family. This opened the path to connection, as Dan then proceeded to contact them one by one, opening a floodgate of questions, feelings, and connections. A network was beginning to spread out before him.

A few months later, Dan flew to Colorado to meet his newly found family. His mom had been diagnosed with Alzheimer's; the disease was progressing, though she was still cognizant of who he was—and that he was her son. She could reconstruct, in bits and pieces, the events surrounding his conception. She explained that while her husband was serving time in prison, she had a brief romantic relationship that resulted in Dan's conception. When he discovered she was pregnant, her husband pressured her to give Dan up for adoption. She ceded, and Dan was adopted by a couple who moved to Western Colorado, then Montana, Alaska, and eventually Iowa. Dan moved to Chicago after grad school.

Over five decades later, Dan discovered his biological mom, reconnected with his siblings, and heard the story of his conception. He was grateful for the conversations they had, and for the new links with his biological family.

A year later, he attended his mom's memorial service. The day of the funeral Dan texted and thanked his friend who had found his mother. She was an instrument of providence, of God's grace, even for the short moment in time that he knew his biological mom.

Dan's adoptive parents were—and are—loving and kind. Nothing was missing there. But still, this discovery was a vivid reminder that he had biological parents and a complicated lineage. A deep and organic connection to humanity.

The logic of the incarnation implies that Jesus is biologically linked with the human species. Jesus could redeem us because he became one of us, *from the inside*, as a humanly conceived person, in the muck and the mire of human history and embodied existence. The early theologians understood the importance of this biological connection. That's why they insisted that Jesus "took flesh" from his mother. Within the framework of contemporary biology, we need to consider whether Jesus had to take something from his father, too.

Not just humanity, but all of life is biologically linked through the long and winding evolutionary line. Denis Edwards argues that the incarnation means that Jesus's humanity was part of creation, not separated from it—nor from us. The divine Son of God joins our evolutionary history in Jesus. Just like us, Jesus's humanity depended "on the hydrogen that formed in the beginning of the universe, on the carbon and the other elements synthesized in stars, and on the long history of evolutionary emergence on Earth."[14] In other words, if you and I are made of stardust, so was Jesus. Peacocke puts it this way: The logic of the incarnation means that "Jesus must be bone of our bone, flesh of our flesh, and DNA of our DNA, DNA from a human father, in order to have any salvific role for humanity."[15]

For these theologians, a virginal conception short-circuits the organic, biological connection of Jesus to the human race. It would have disconnected Jesus from the evolutionary line of humanity—and indeed from all of life, beginning with the first primordial cell. A virgin-born Jesus would be a different kind of human being from you and from me. At the very least, it implies that God's involvement in the conception of Jesus of Nazareth was strikingly different than God's involvement in yours and mine.

I hope you can sense it. The pressure builds as we pursue this journey still further. For the incarnation to be an *in-fleshing* of the Son of God as Jesus of Nazareth, he had to have been a unique human. But he cannot have been less than human.

The beauty of the incarnation unfolds before us. In Jesus Christ, the divine Son of God became the "exact imprint of God's very being" as a human being (Hebrews 1:3). He lived with us, as one of us: flesh, blood, bone, brain, and DNA. He revealed God's nature to us by and in his human life (John 1:11). The divine Son of God entered our evolutionary history, with all its splendors, banalities, and sufferings. He invites us to join in the healing and redemption of creation.

While I'm not ready to answer whether Jesus was really born of a virgin, I can say this: Surely the incarnation of the Son of God in human history didn't *require* a miraculous beginning. That doesn't mean the incarnation itself wasn't a miracle, even if the conception that began Jesus's life was natural and involved both a biological mother and father. If Jesus Christ, the divine Son of God, were conceived by human procreation, he was no less God's gift to the world.

THE MOST NATURAL OCCURRENCES ARE SOMETIMES OUR GREATEST MIRACLES

Scientists don't traffic in miracle stories. In the context of their work at least, they rely on natural explanations. Nonetheless, creation so often *seems* miraculous for its beauty, spontaneity, and marvels of nature. The universe reminds us that we should remain open to the possibility of rare, unusual, and unexpected things.

The British philosopher David Hume (1711–1776) defined a miracle as a "violation of the laws of nature."[16] For Hume, and for many philosophers and theologians since, an event only counts as a miracle if nature's laws are clearly interrupted or disrupted by a supernatural intervention. Many people use the term a lot more flexibly these days. A Packers fan exclaims, "A miracle!" when Aaron Rodgers tosses a last-second Hail Mary touchdown pass to win the game. (A Vikings fan calls it something else.) An unemployed single mom about to lose her home to foreclosure finds an envelope of cash from an anonymous donor: "Miracle!" Winning the Powerball lottery would feel like a miracle to most of us, even though everyone knows it's just dumb luck. The surprising nature of an event often gives rise to the miracle label because of the joy or surprise involved.

BABY ZOEY: A MIRACLE OF SCIENCE?

My friends Rachael and Joel had tried unsuccessfully for seven years to get pregnant. They eventually learned that Rachael suffered from endometriosis, a condition that displaces the tissue that normally lines the inside of the uterus, often causing infertility. They began to discuss the possibility of in vitro fertilization (IVF), a medical process in which eggs are extracted from a woman's ovary, are mixed with a man's sperm (insemination), and are stored in a laboratory, awaiting hoped-for fertilization.

IVF is a lengthy, elaborate, and costly process. Rachael and Joel struggled with the decision to go through with it, primarily for humanitarian reasons. Should they invest their financial resources into having their own biological child when they could adopt a child who was already born; or alternatively, adopt an already-formed embryo that could then be implanted into Rachael? They decided to go through with the full process of IVF, thereby joining Rachael's eggs and Joel's sperm in a very nonromantic way—in a petri dish. They believed that God intended to bless their desire to have their own biological child.

Their first cycle of IVF resulted in the successful fertilization of twins, but there was a serious complication: the twins were conjoined. Joel and Rachael then made the challenging decision of following through with the pregnancy in the aftermath of that news, and committing to care for the twins if they had life. Sadly, the twins miscarried prior to full term. Despite the grave disappointment and amid the challenges, Joel and Rachael kept trying. After two lengthy and costly cycles of IVF, they finally had a fertilized egg that resulted in a pregnancy and the birth of a healthy newborn baby girl, whom they named Zoey (*zoe* is Greek for *life*).

Their journey to a family was different from most. IVF is certainly not a typical conception process. But at the pivotal moment, IVF is no different from any other pregnancy: a sperm meets an egg and fertilizes the egg to form the embryo that becomes a living, breathing child. And most importantly, for Joel and Rachael, while their pregnancy wasn't typical, it was still natural. It happened through biological, scientific, technological processes that scientists and doctors thoroughly understand.

The technology of the science of reproduction forces us to reconsider what's "normal." For Rachael and Joel, the birth of Zoey, after a lengthy and expensive process of trial and error, including much prayer, many close calls, and many disappointments, is a gift from God. Precious Zoey would not be alive, she would not be their daughter, apart from medical technology. And yet, they believe that God was involved in the process and in their lives at every point on the way.

I recently asked Rachael whether the birth of Zoey felt like a miracle. She said no. It seemed more like science: mechanistic, technical, structured; lots of trial and error.

They conceived their second child, Soren, the old-fashioned way; and he was a surprise baby. Rachael only discovered she was pregnant two months into the pregnancy. Perhaps ironically, to Rachael and Joel, Soren did feel like a miracle, primarily because of the unplanned nature of the occurrence and because the odds were very low that Rachael would get pregnant naturally.

Zoey's conception was meticulously planned, strategized, and rendered possible through the implementation or application of high-level technological and scientific knowledge. Nonetheless, she transformed their lives for the better: she brought them love, happiness, and an expanded family. They believe she is a gift from God, through the technicalities and technologies of science. But Soren's birth, so typical and natural, had a hint of the miraculous. No intervention, no artificial insemination, no regular medication, no statistical planning. Just real, normal, human intercourse. But equally a divine gift from God.

Maybe we've been thinking of the conception of Jesus in the wrong way. The traditional notion of the virgin birth, which can seem like a "divine artificial insemination," might turn out to be less remarkable than the alternative: real, human sex as the mechanism for the incarnation. Imagine the possibility! A human procreative act led to a nonetheless surprising gift: the unique presence of God in human history, the redemption of the world, the resurrection of life over death.

Maybe, just maybe. But there's more to consider —including "the problem of Mary," the mother of Jesus.

NOTES

1. http://news.nationalgeographic.com/2015/06/
   150601-virgin-birth-animals-sawfish-endangered-
   genetics-science/.

2. http://news.nationalgeographic.com/news/2007/05/
   070524-shark-virgin.html.

3. http://news.nationalgeographic.com/news/2008/10/
   081010-shark-virgin-birth-2.html.

4. http://news.nationalgeographic.com/2015/06/
   150601-virgin-birth-animals-sawfish-endangered-
   genetics-science/.

5. Aarathi Prasad, *Like a Virgin: How Science Is Redesigning the Rules of Sex* (Oxford: Oneworld, 2012), 85.

6. The U.S. Department of Agriculture discovered a group of turkeys, named the "Beltsville Small White Breed," laying eggs asexually (parthenogenically) and found that several different viruses stimulated asexual reproduction. See Prasad, *Like a Virgin*, 95–96.

7. Origen, *Against Celsus*, in Alexander Roberts and James Donaldson, eds., *The Ante-Nicene Fathers*, 10 vols. (Buffalo, NY: Christian Literature, 1885–1896; Reprint, Grand Rapids, MI: Eerdmans, 1951–1956; Reprint, Peabody, MA: Hendrickson, 1994), vol. 4, 2.6.438.

8. For a fascinating discussion of how Mary might have conceived virginally (from a scientific perspective), see Aarathi Prasad's summary of Sam Berry's thought experiment in *Like a Virgin*, 80–84.

9. Charles Augustus Briggs, "The Virgin Birth of Our Lord," *The American Journal of Theology* 12, no. 2 (1908): 189–210, 206.

10. Arthur Peacocke, *Theology for a Scientific Age: Being and Becoming—Natural, Divine, and Human* (Minneapolis: Fortress Press, 1993), 276.

11. Peacocke, *Theology for a Scientific Age*, 277.

12. Augustine says, "Christ took the visible substance of his flesh from the Virgin's flesh; but the principle of his conception did not spring from the seed of man." *Gen. litt.* 10.20. Cited in Andrew Lincoln, *Born of a Virgin? Reconceiving Jesus in the Bible, Tradition, and Theology* (Grand Rapids, MI: Eerdmans, 2013), 283. Also, Athanasius writes that the Son of God "took flesh of a Virgin, Mary Bearer of God, and was man." *Four Discourses Against the Arians*, in Philip Schaff et al., eds., *The Nicene and Post-Nicene Fathers* (Buffalo, NY: Christian Literature, 1886–98: Reprint Peabody, MA: Hendrickson, 1996), vol. 4, 409.

13. Gregory of Nazianzus, "To Cledonius the Priest Against Apollinarius," in Schaff et al., eds., *The Nicene and Post-Nicene Fathers*, vol. 7, 440.

14. Denis Edwards, *How God Acts: Creation, Redemption, and Special Divine Action* (Minneapolis: Fortress Press, 2010), 74.

15. Peacocke, *Theology for a Scientific Age*, 278.

16. David Hume, *An Enquiry Concerning Human Understanding*, ed. Anthony Flew (Chicago: Open Court, 1988), 148.

4

THE MOST POWERFUL WOMAN IN THE WORLD

National Geographic's December 2015 issue featured a cover story about Mary titled "How the Virgin Mary Became the World's Most Powerful Woman."[1] The piece had little to do with the Gospels or with early nonbiblical legends about Mary. It explored how the symbol and persona of Mary has been received throughout the world: the adoration, wonder, and love she has garnered for 2,000 years and counting. In the Christian imagination, Mary was a special recipient of divine grace and a receptacle of a supernatural miracle; but her blessings and her influence didn't stop with her role as the mother of Jesus. Christians all over the world—and Muslims, too—revere Mary as a special religious figure. For many Catholic believers, Mary is the *Mediatrix* of salvation, interceding on behalf of humanity for Jesus's saving grace.

People across the globe believe Mary performs miracles. She makes angelic appearances through visions and dreams, in images and impressions (with varying levels of ambiguity and clarity); her visage appears in clouds, in stone, in soup, on trees, on clothes, even in pizza. *Pizza?*

But to some convinced believers, she shows up and speaks. Many of these visionaries (recipients of Mary's appearances) believe that the mother of God prayed specifically for them, pronounced a blessing on their behalf, prophesied forthcoming tragedies, or performed other miracles. Some believe they've been healed by Mary; others that they've been empowered, encouraged, and given hope to endure suffering or oppression. The Vatican has a special division of experts that investigates claims of Mary's miracles; some 2,000 sightings of Mary have been reported or claimed since 40 CE. Twelve of those have been formally recognized by the Vatican as bona fide miracles.

I'm skeptical about such claims, but I can't deny

that Mary is seen by many Christians to be a symbol of empowerment and divine grace in female form. As the "mother of God," "God-bearer" (*Theotokos*), "Queen of Heaven," "Madonna," and other grand titles, her gravitas and authority can hardly be overstated. Many encounter Mary, along with Jesus Christ, as a salvific and revelatory figure; though not equal with God, she nonetheless heals, liberates, and inspires. She shows up most vividly in places of hardship and to people in vulnerable or desperate situations.

The Feast of Our Lady of Guadalupe, one of the most important religious celebrations in Mexico, commemorates the appearance of Mary to a poor peasant man named Juan Diego in 1531, a decade after Indian Mexico was conquered by Spain.[2] The Virgin appeared to Diego and beckoned him to go to the archbishop of Mexico and tell him to build a temple on the site of her appearance, so Mary could "communicate all her love, compassion, help, and defense to all the inhabitants of this land."[3] As proof of her intentions, Mary then performed a miracle: blooming roses in the desert, and manifesting her image on Diego's cloak as he presented the gathered roses to the archbishop.

Virgilio Elizondo says that these miracles were only the beginning of the wonders of Mary's works for the Mexican people. The "real miracle" wasn't the apparition itself, but the empowerment felt by the conquered Indian. Those who "had been robbed of their lands and of their way of life and even of their gods were now coming to life. They who had been silenced were now speaking again through the voice of the Lady. They who wanted only to die now wanted to live."[4]

The impact of the apparition went beyond existential courage to a tangible and political hope. The Mexican people drew enormous strength from the story of Mary's appearance to a simple peasant man. They carried her image through wars, political revolutions, and labor strikes. "She is the symbol of *la raza*, the definition of what it means to be Mexican, and because of Our Lady of Guadalupe, Mexicans have always believed they're special."[5] The apparition gave rise to a renewed sense of hope and contributed to a vibrant Mexican identity, one that quickly spread among the people and continues to endear the mother of Jesus to so many of them.

The story of the Virgin of Guadalupe exemplifies the tension that comes when we consider Mary today. Traditional theologians admire her virginity and purity, her motherhood, and her submissiveness to God's calling. But there's more to Mary than meets the patriarchal eye. Mary's appearances, miracles of healing, prophetic pronouncements, and words of empowerment inspire political revolution and social liberation.

Much of the Christian theological tradition across the world continues to pigeonhole women as valuable for their bodies, for their sexuality (and especially for their virginal status), for their "innate" capabilities of motherhood, and for their submissiveness or obedience. Despite the adulation, Christianity too often holds Mary captive in the grips of patriarchy.

THE PROBLEM OF MARY

After I graduated from college, I lived for a year in Tegucigalpa, Honduras, teaching in a private school for Honduran nationals. To celebrate Holy Week (*Semana Santa*), my colleague, Steve, and I ventured to Antigua, Guatemala. For most the year, Antigua is a nondescript, quaint village. But during Holy Week thousands of Guatemalans descend upon the town and take part in an elaborate festival, which involves laying down brightly covered, meticulous patterns of beads and flowers on the roads. After the roads and walkways are covered solid with color, the main event begins: a parade of hand-held floats, beginning with one dedicated to the Virgin Mary, carried from the steps of the main church in the square throughout the streets of the village. From Ash Wednesday through Good Friday, this solemn procession winds through the streets. Somber worshippers trample the intricate patterns of flowers to dust. But no matter: that was the point.

Next to the beauty of the celebration, I remember most vividly the dirty and dingy hotel room we stayed in. Upon entering our room, we did our best to peel the hairs from the sheets—there were no clean ones available. We did convince the manager to remove the dead bat from the room. This was our consequence for not prebooking: our own pseudo infancy narrative moment. We got the very last room in the very last inn, for there was no room for us in the others. When we woke up the next morning, all unpleasantness faded in the light of the Guatemalan sun. Just outside the door, pathways of color and religious devotion opened before us.

I recall trying to wrap my mind around the exaltation of Mary; she appeared on every float and in every display. This seemed unusual, to me, especially during a week meant to celebrate Good Friday. In a Christmas festival, this would have made perfect sense, given Mary's role in the birth of Jesus. But Mary's prominence seemed out of place, since she plays only a small role in the Passion narratives. As a U.S. evangelical Protestant, I didn't yet fully appreciate the importance of Mary in the larger Christian imagination. But there I was, face-to-face with the mother of the son of God in a dusty, bustling, Guatemalan town.

Symbols and statues can only say so much. Her constant, dutiful appearance in churches, in nativities, on floats, does not yet tell us what Mary *does* for us—especially for women. The many patriarchal systems of Christianity across the world create dissonance between the deep reverence for Mary on the one hand, and the unjust subjugation, marginalization, and even abusive treatment of women, on the other.

The feminist theologian Mary Daly (1928–2010) suggests that the Catholic tradition offered the mother of Jesus as something of a peace offering to women; Daly calls this a "compensatory glory."[6] The high regard for Mary stands as the exception to an otherwise thoroughly masculinized religion: a male-authored Bible, male-dominated theology and creeds, a male-led institutional church, and a male Savior. Apart from Mary, it's penises all the way down. So, thank God for Mary. Even if Christians often subordinate her to the "male" figures and masculine images that dominate Christian affection and worship: Father, Jesus—and sadly, many Christians even think of the Holy Spirit as a male. But Mary's constant presence in Catholic churches and cathedrals reminds us that God's redemptive plan includes the female.[7]

But that concession doesn't offset the "problem of Mary" created by male dominance in Christian traditions. Feminist theologians draw our attention to the ways in which the patriarchal structure of Christianity continues to revere Mary while simultaneously denigrating and objectifying women, often based at least in part on their "authoritative" interpretations of the virgin birth accounts.

The traditional Christian approach to Mary sets up a no-win situation for women. On the one hand, the virgin birth accounts inspire reverence for traditionally feminine roles: motherhood, nurturing, receptivity, submission. But the rug is pulled out from under women who seek to conform to traditional roles because they can't possibly measure up to the ideal exemplified by the traditional symbol of Mary. Standard, authoritative treatments of the virgin birth stories overlook Mary's humanity and idealize her beyond human recognition. They valorize the unrepeatable supernatural divine conception, the offensive notion of the bloodless and painless birth, and they hold up the perpetual virginity of Mary as the highest ideal for women. Far from an attainable example for both women and men, the Mary of the dominant Christian imagination can come across as an abnormal mythic figure. She's given a special and unusual divine grace but saddled with a burdensome responsibility. "Mary is glorified but presented as an impossible model."[8]

Christian theologians have often valorized virginity and undermined sexuality, especially female sexuality. Recall our discussion of Jerome's emphasis on virginity as a Christian vocation. For Jerome, the best thing about a Christian marriage is the chance that the couple might produce offspring who become lifelong Christian virgins![9] For Daly and others, this has contributed to a structure in the Catholic Church that inscribes and perpetuates male headship, an all-male priesthood, and the supremacy of celibacy, thereby also downgrading human sexuality and treating the female body with ambivalence.

While the virgin Mary has often empowered women to claim their sexuality and identity *apart* from relationships with men, the institutional church too often renders her a tool for male dominance.[10] Mary's assertiveness, inspiration for liberation, and healing power are often overshadowed by other images—the glorified church and the submissive bride who meets up with Christ in heaven.[11]

The emphasis on female submissiveness also contributes to a culture that too often tolerates violence against women.

DIVINE RAPE?

Western culture seems far removed from the patriarchy and brutality of first-century Palestine. Nonetheless, violence plagues every age and every culture. It's a common human problem, especially oppression by the powerful against the vulnerable. In the United States, violence against women sometimes occurs prominently on university campuses.

Headlines suggest the presence in some campus settings of a fertile ground for violence against women; sexism and misogyny in athletic programs and in fraternity life, or a party culture more generally. In the past few years, two large universities—the University of Minnesota and Baylor University —experienced tumult in their athletic programs for allegations of rape against female students by student-athletes.

We've come to expect such stories out of secular universities, but scandals at self-identifying Christian schools elicit special consternation.[12] A journalist noted the irony of an avowed Christian university allowing a sexist and violent culture to fester, referencing an investigation that "found a culture where victims who came forward found themselves blamed for violating the university's code of con-duct, which prohibits drinking and premarital sex."[13]

A bias against victims, especially female victims, continues to haunt our social institutions, including the church. Victims and potential victims of sexual assault often receive a message that it's their fault: they shouldn't have taken that last shot of Vodka, they shouldn't have worn those clothes, they shouldn't have been at the party in the first place. Rather than blaming the perpetrators or the systems that generate cycles of violence and abuse against vulnerable persons, many people blame the victim.

From a contemporary vantage point the virgin birth accounts raise tough questions about this state of affairs. Since Mary was probably twelve to four-teen years old (and almost surely not older than eigh-teen) at the time of the conception of Jesus, there is a question of consent. Given her young age, and the improbability of a young girl declining a request by a divine messenger to make her body available to God, the accounts could imply something like a "divine rape" of Mary. What does it mean that the "power of the Most High will overshadow you" (Luke 1:35)? What are we to make of Mary's reply to the angel's announcement: "Here am I, the servant of the Lord; let it be with me according to your word" (Luke 1:38)? Could Mary have said No?

Neither Matthew nor Luke explicitly suggests physical contact between the Holy Spirit and Mary. Nonetheless, God's messenger appears with no warning to a young, poor, peasant girl who had been taught all her life the importance of obeying Yahweh. He announces that God will make her pregnant and that she will give birth to the Messiah. Yes, she consents; but still, it comes off as the ultimate power differential. I've heard many eloquent sermons that marvel at Mary's obedience to God: she answered Yes to God's request. But there's no request in the text: just an announcement, a divine proclamation. Even if Mary could have said no to the angel, it's hard to imagine that she would have denied the God she had been trained all her life to obey.

Perhaps that's reading too much contemporary sensibility into an ancient text, in a context when Mary would have been considered of age and marriageable. The angel promised that Mary was chosen to carry the Christ child, and that the birth of Jesus would bless not just her, but the world. While it's appropriate to raise the question of consent in the infancy narratives, Luke offers another avenue to explore. In the *Magnificat*, which I earlier called "Mary's Freedom Song," Mary seized an opportunity, with full awareness of all the ways it would also empower her to participate in the liberation of her people and in the salvation of the world.

But for growing numbers of people today, rightly sensitized to the problem of sexual violence and to the objectification of women and girls, the virgin birth story evokes a coerced, instrumental use of a woman's body; a forced pregnancy—a power differential of infinite proportions: a young girl impregnated by the creator of the universe. From this perspective, the virgin birth story is at the least an archaic and primitive reflection of a patriarchal society that was routinely oppressive toward women. At the most, it's yet another sacred text useful for ongoing perpetuation of injustice, degradation, and harm to women. This reading of the infancy narratives coupled with the traditional theology of Mary shows that the infancy narratives can and have been used to continue to support patriarchy, to suppress gender equality, and to underwrite sexual and emotional abuse against women.

Today, the idealized virginal conception seems like a leftover from a primitive worldview. It portrays female sexuality differently from male sexuality and treats virginity as a commodity, an ideal useful for some "higher" purpose, but a purpose not of women's own choosing or making. And this is detrimental to healthy attitudes about the human body and sexuality.

Much of the conservative Christian culture in the U.S. still places a premium on sexual purity and identifies purity with chastity. In the conservative evangelical church of my youth, I heard lots of youth group pep talks, stern warnings, and testimonials about chastity. There's something admirable and important about that impulse. Conservative Christian approaches to sexuality can teach people the art of discipline and encourage delayed gratification. They recognize and inspire moral seriousness. And, for those who follow the admonitions, sexual fidelity undergirds commitment and can contribute to healthy, durable marriages.

But what I picked up in youth group was this: Besides "accepting Jesus as my personal savior," nothing was more important than sexual chastity. Fidelity, commitment, and discipline are laudable and integral to the Christian tradition and to spiritual disciplines. Nonetheless, if ministers took seriously the Gospels' portrayal of Jesus, they would spend more time and energy encouraging young people to think about justice, cultivating a heart of compassion toward the marginalized and oppressed, and practicing love of neighbor. Jesus rarely mentioned sex, but he talked a lot about justice and compassion, serving the poor and the prisoner, and standing in solidarity with the oppressed. He shone a light of righteousness on the hypocrisy of the Pharisees, who extolled the letter of the law over the spirit of the law.

For many people today, sexuality isn't viewed through the idealized or purity-mindset of times past. The traditional belief that God chose virginal conception as the entry point for the incarnation shouldn't be based on an idealized view of sexuality, especially one derived from a patriarchal mindset. The patriarchy of Christianity's origins often considered women the property of men and as essentially inferior to men. While they elevated female sexual chastity, they seemed comparatively less concerned about male sexual practice. It's true that early theologians do include male biblical figures as models of virginity and of sexual chastity, including Jesus and, occasionally, Joseph too. Furthermore, virginity was valued as a religious calling for men, too. But overall, traditional Christianity inordinately objectifies female sexuality. Whatever our answer to the question whether Jesus was born of a virgin, we need a better approach to Mary.

The Gospel accounts don't just give us a domestic Mary, a stereotypically feminine maiden whose primary value is her body, her sexual availability, and her capacity for motherhood. Mary, particularly in Luke's account, is receptive to God but she's also subversive and assertive. She seizes on the words of the messenger and makes use of the moment in a powerful way. God gives her a chance to participate in a central way in the redemption of her people Israel in the context of political and social oppression. God humbles the mighty and uplifts the oppressed and the vulnerable. She assumes a central role in the reclamation of her people, the overthrowing of empires and evils, and in the salvation of the world. She becomes not just mother of Jesus, but partner to the Messiah, the king who will set his people free. Far from a helpless victim of patriarchy, Mary—like Jesus—overturns its tables.

A WOMAN NEEDS A MAN LIKE A FISH NEEDS A BICYCLE

When you look closely enough, you can't miss the patriarchal elements of the virgin birth—especially in how later theologians interpreted the Gospel stories. But don't throw the (virgin birth) baby out with the bathwater just yet! Some feminist theologians see the infancy narratives as a challenge to patriarchy because they elevate the role of a woman in salvation history.

I once discussed the question of the virgin birth with a female theologian. When I raised the problem of patriarchy in the virgin birth, her response surprised me:

> *The virgin birth is the one place where Christianity elevates the stature of a* woman. *Jesus Christ gets his flesh from Mary—not from Joseph. From a woman, not from a man. Now all these contemporary theologians want to shove Mary aside and put a man (presumably Joseph) right there alongside her—or perhaps over her. Let us have Mary—at least!*

She urged me not to mess with the manger scene because the infancy narratives put a female figure at the center. Why mess with that?

My theologian friend is certainly not alone in this feeling.

The biblical authors likely had a more liberating picture in mind than the one drawn through so much Christian history. As the mother of Jesus and the main character in the first few chapters of Matthew and Luke, Mary stands out in vivid color. She gives Christianity a strong and vibrant female

figure in many of the traditions, liturgies, and celebrations of the church.

We can read the infancy narratives as empowering women in the context of patriarchy—so long as
we read them with an eye toward liberation.[14] Janice
Capel Anderson sees Mary as a heroic figure, occu-
pying a central role in the story of salvation.[15] "God
has acted in a radically new way—outside of the
patriarchal norm. Although Jesus is Son of David
through Joseph, he is Son of God through Mary."[16]
For Anderson, the Gospel narratives reveal an
equally high reverence for Mary as for Jesus.

Similarly, Elizabeth Wainwright points to the
absence of a male in the conception of Jesus as an
affirmation of the "reproductive power of woman"
beyond the structures of patriarchy.[17] And Elizabeth
Johnson reminds us that despite the uses and abuses
by patriarchy of Mary and the virgin birth, the story
has empowered countless women and other marginalized persons for liberation and for spiritual
vibrancy throughout history.[18]

But to find this empowering Mary, she must arise
from the rubble of patriarchy. To paraphrase Gloria
Steinem and U2, *God needed a man like a fish needs a
bicycle.* The virginal conception bypassed the procreative role of the human male, signaling that the salvation of humanity would come not via a patriarchal

genealogy and as result of male biology, but through a peasant girl blessed by the power of God's spirit.

You've got to admit: That's a compelling way to look at the virgin birth story!

There's an interesting—if surprising—analogue here to Augustine's argument that the virgin birth protected Jesus from the consequences of original sin. Taking the male parent out of the picture disrupted the transmission of original sin, thereby protecting Jesus from its consequences. The virginal conception shielded Jesus from the sin and guilt that impacts the rest of us.

In an analogous way, one feminist reading of the virgin birth story emphasizes that the conception of Jesus bypasses the male father; only the human mother really matters. Many feminist scholars probably don't read the virgin birth accounts literally, but reconstructively, as stories that contribute to a theology that values women on their own terms. Read with a bias toward the liberation of women (and yes, we all have biases!) the vulnerable girl stands up in the context of an overwhelmingly patriarchal world. Mary's "yes" to God came in response to God's "yes" to Mary—an affirmation that women would play a significant role in the story of God's salvation. God liberates Mary; in turn, Mary participates in the liberation of the oppressed and victimized of the world.

The Bible includes a liberating impulse but one that has often been neglected or suppressed, the result of blind spots of male theologians who have largely shaped the meaning of the Bible for "authorized" versions of Christianity. A recovery reading helps us see what is so often neglected in Scripture, as well as in Jesus's own life and relationship to women. In the Gospels, Jesus often counteracted patriarchy. He used his influence to affirm the role of women in his inner circle and even scandalously spoke with women in public, such as the Samaritan woman at the well (John 4:1–42). We can read the stories of the beginning of Jesus's life in this light—with new attention to Mary as an assertive, creative woman who seized her opportunity.

There's another feminist angle to explore: the role of the Holy Spirit in the birth of Jesus. In the infancy narratives, the Holy Spirit conceived in Mary (Luke 1:35; Matthew 1:18). God the Father wasn't the divine procreator; the Gospels name the Spirit as the agent of conception. But here's where it gets interesting: Later Christian tradition articulated the Holy Spirit as the third person of the Trinity: fully and completely divine, but with a distinct personhood. Some groups within early Christianity thought of the Spirit as the "feminine" person of the Trinity, representing stereotypically feminine characteristics, such as creating, nurturing, guiding, convicting. They addressed the Spirit in liturgical worship with female pronouns: as "she" and "her." Consider the example of Aphrahat, a third-century Syriac-Christian monk who wrote: "By baptism we receive the Spirit of Christ, and at that moment when the priests invoke the Spirit, she opens the heavens and descends and hovers over the waters, and those who are baptized put her on."[19]

I'm speculating now, but it's intriguing to imagine that, even within the framework of the traditional account of the virginal conception, something surprising was happening: God bypassed the male in the procreation of Jesus, emphasizing instead the role of the female, and interacting with Mary in that procreative act through the Holy Spirit. We could also read the story as an upending of the patriarchal family structure, with a "feminine" Spirit conceiving in a virginal mother, absent the role of a biological father. As Amy-Jill Levine puts it, Jesus was born into a family "not ruled by or even defined by a male head of the house."[20]

Since the biblical accounts leave out any explicit suggestion of sexual procreative action, we have little grounds to seriously consider that Jesus was the offspring of a lesbian, divine-human procreative act. It's also problematic to exclusively associate any of the Trinitarian persons with distinctive gender characteristics, or to assume that gender characteristics are fixed and clearly defined on a spectrum. Nonetheless, it illustrates how the virgin birth accounts can be read through the lens of their ambiguity, blurred boundaries, and creative potential, rather than as perpetuating hierarchy and sexism.

A DIFFERENT MARY FOR
A BETTER HUMANITY

We can interpret the infancy narratives to serve the liberation of women from patriarchal oppression; nonetheless, we still must take note of the patriarchy and sexism endemic to the traditional approach to the virgin birth stories. Reading the biblical texts afresh and anew gives us a better vision of Mary. And it allows us to take dominant Christian patriarchy to task—which is always fun!

Mary is neither the impossible ideal nor a unique recipient of supernatural grace. Nor is she merely a disembodied virginal vessel of God's miraculous procreative action. She's the real, flesh-and-blood mother of Jesus who experienced God's empowerment in the context of vulnerability and hope in the face of evil. The Gospels announce that God does a new thing in and through Jesus and through this young Jewish mother—and yes, through Joseph, too. But this new thing subverts oppressive patriarchy, by shining a bright light on this peasant girl in God's salvation story.

Throughout this book, we've been exploring the question of the virgin birth through reflection on the incarnation. Inadequate theologies of the incarnation separate Jesus's divinity from his humanity and prioritize the divine Son of God over the human Jesus of Nazareth—eclipsing his humanity in the process. A similar thing has happened to Mary. The veneration of Mary can render her *more than* human—or at the least an extremely unusual person. Christianity too often presents Mary as a mythic figure, an unattainable ideal, and implies that female embodiment is inherently problematic.

I affirm, along with the Christian tradition, that Mary was the "God-Bearer" (or, if you prefer, the "Christ-Bearer") and the mother of the Messiah, but I do so with caveats. She was a person who claimed her agency and took her place in the flow of God's historical, political, spiritual, and social salvation. But she lived in a flawed world, beset by many evils. A genuine theology of the incarnation must consider the human origin of Jesus of Nazareth, but it also must explore the meaning and significance of Mary. Doing so gives us a more liberating and more human gospel. But to go one step further, we need to dig more into the biblical texts themselves and explore what they might—or might not—say to the question still at hand: Was Jesus really born of a virgin?

NOTES

1. http://ngm.nationalgeographic.com/2015/12/virgin-mary-text.

2. Virgilio Elizondo, *Galilean Journey: The Mexican-American Promise* (Maryknoll, NY: Orbis, 2006), 11–12.

3. Ibid., 11.

4. Ibid.

5. http://ngm.nationalgeographic.com/2015/12/virgin-mary-text.

6. Mary Daly, *Beyond God the Father: Toward a Philosophy of Women's Liberation*, revised version (Boston: Beacon, 1985), 81.

7. Tissa Balasuriya, *Mary and Human Liberation: The Story and the Text* (Harrisburg, PA: Trinity), 155.

8. Rosemary Radford Ruether, *Sexism and God-Talk: Toward a Feminist Theology*, revised edition (Boston: Beacon, 1993), 155.

9. Ruether, *Sexism and God-Talk*, 143.

10. Daly, *Beyond God the Father*, 155.

11. Ruether, *Sexism and God-Talk*, 149–50.

12. http://www.cbsnews.com/news/baylor-official-addresses-mishandled-sexual-assault-allegation-against-star-football-player/.

13. http://www.cbsnews.com/news/baylor-official-addresses-mishandled-sexual-assault-allegation-against-star-football-player/.

14. As Amy-Jill Levine writes, "The combination of the feminine Spirit and Jesus' lack of a human father . . . continues the theme of restructuring the family to decrease paternal importance." "Gospel of Matthew," in *Women's Bible Commentary, Third Edition; Revised and Updated*, ed. Carol A. Newsom, Sharon H. Ringe, and Jacqueline E. Lapsey (Louisville: Westminster John Knox, 2012), 468.

15. Janice Capel Anderson, "Matthew: Gender and Reading," in *A Feminist Companion to Matthew*, ed. Amy-Jill Levine (Sheffield: Sheffield Academic, 2001), 25–51, 10.

16. Anderson, "Matthew: Gender and Reading," 10.

17. Elizabeth Wainwright, "The Gospel of Matthew," in *Searching the Scriptures*, II. *A Feminist Commentary*, ed. Elisabeth Schüssler Fiorenza (New York: Crossroad, 1994), 643.

18. Elizabeth Johnson, *Truly Our Sister: A Theology of Mary in the Communion of Saints* (New York: Continuum, 2003).

19. Aphrahat, *Demonstration* 6:14. Cited in Clark Pinnock, *Flame of Love: A Theology of the Holy Spirit* (Downers Grove, IL: InterVarsity, 1996), 16.

20. Levine, "Gospel of Matthew," 254.

5

A
CONTROVERSIAL
AND
TOO-SILENT
NIGHT

In 2008, at the height of Barack Obama's presidential campaign, conspiracy theorists raised a ruckus when they claimed Obama was not a natural-born U.S. citizen. If true and proven, this accusation would have nullified his candidacy for president under Article Two of the Constitution. There were several versions of the theory, but most claimed that Obama's birth certificate was a forgery. Donald Trump was an outspoken and unrelenting proponent of the most popular claim: that Obama was born in Kenya (his father's birthplace) rather than Hawaii. Others suggested that he became an Indonesian citizen in childhood, and still others insisted he'd been born a dual citizen of the U.S. and Great Britain. These theories persisted throughout much of Obama's presidency. Even the release of Obama's birth certificate, including the 2011 release of a long-form version, didn't completely squelch the theory, although it named Hawaii as his birthplace and the Hawaii Department of Health confirmed its legitimacy. Trump didn't retract his claim until September 2016, near the end of his own successful bid for the presidency. He followed up his retraction with a new accusation: Hilary Clinton, Trump's political opponent, started the rumor about Obama.

Birth stories may not be as important as they used to be, but for some purposes they still matter a great deal. In the U.S., a national birth (born on U.S. soil) establishes the baseline requirement for admission to the highest office in the land. That requirement for legitimacy has created the opportunity for some very high-profile challenges to authority. Rumors like the "birther" conspiracy are effective because it's difficult to prove something from the past. Simply raising a question like, "How can we be *sure* Obama's birth certificate wasn't forged?," however far-fetched or unfounded it might be, stokes the fires of skepticism. Lies, cover-ups, and fabrications are common and can be easily perpetuated by those in positions of power. On the other hand, people also understand that conspiracy theories themselves are often lies and falsehoods, sometimes based on "alternative facts," intended to fan the flames of controversy and to confirm the biases already at work in people's imaginations, whether those biases are motivated by racism and prejudice, political affiliation, religious ideology, or psychological imbalance.

The prevalence of conspiracy theories reminds us that it's difficult to establish the truth of history. When prejudice or malicious intent enters the picture, it's damn near impossible.

Which brings us to the Bible.

A CONSPICUOUS ABSENCE

The story of the virgin birth of Jesus appears in only two of the four Gospels: Matthew 1:18–25 and Luke 1:26–2:21. There's no direct mention of a virginal conception anywhere else in Scripture.

Neither Mark nor John has an infancy narrative and neither includes any mention of a virgin birth, nor anything about Jesus's birth or childhood at all.

John's prologue (John 1:1–18) refers to Jesus being the "word" (*logos*) with God who existed prior to the creation of the world. But the story of Jesus's human life in John begins with his baptism by John the Baptist. Mark begins his Gospel with an adult Jesus, too: the baptism launches Jesus into his public ministry. The New Testament doesn't mention the virgin birth anywhere else. The Book of Revelation alludes to a woman pregnant with a child (Revelation 12:1–2), but there's no hint there of a virginal conception. When Christians all over the world read, hear, or preach the Christmas story, they do so using the accounts from Matthew and Luke, with some folkloric elaborations tossed in, too. The two stories are often conflated in our imaginations; it's difficult to separate them.

My daughter Ella got a bracelet kit for her fifth birthday. The kit includes colored yarn that can be twisted together to make fancy string bracelets. The problem is, those threads have a knack for intertwining themselves—even while they're lying all alone in the box. It's my job to untangle those infernal strings from each other so they can be made into pretty bracelets again. It's a real exercise in patience and sanctification, a good Saturday-morning task for dear old Dad.

Not to be left out, my son Luke went through

a Slinky-loving phase, and Slinkies have a natural ability to wrap their coils around each other in the most fantastically heinous ways. Those things are manufactured with one purpose in mind: testing the patience of parents. Thinking back on it now, the job of a parent consists largely of untangling things —both literally and figuratively.

The biblical accounts and the traditions that creep in from outside the Bible have a way of getting tangled, also. While I can't possibly untie all the threads and coils, I'll have to pull some of them apart. We need to get down to the basics: the question of the historicity of the virgin birth.

No one knows for sure when Matthew and Luke were written, but scholars generally place them somewhere in the timeframe of 80–100 CE, a generation (fifty to seventy years) after Jesus's death. Luke was probably composed later than Matthew. Some scholars place them approximately ten to twenty years after Mark, and ten to twenty years prior to John.[1] They were composed using a combination of oral testimony (stories about Jesus and his teachings that had been told and retold through the Jewish-Christian communities) and various written sources. These sources include the Hebrew Bible —what Christians commonly call the Old Testament—and its translation into Greek, called the

Septuagint. They also used other texts that circulated among early Christian communities; these texts told stories about Jesus's teaching and his life—especially the "passion" narrative of his death and resurrection.

The question of the relationships between the four Gospels is complex. Theories abound about which came first, which made use of the others, and whether any of them were independent of the others. I take the position, along with most biblical scholars today, that Mark is the earliest Gospel, and that both Matthew and Luke borrowed from Mark in composing their Gospels.

Had the virginal conception really happened, and had it been widely known—even if just among the merry band of Jesus followers—it's reasonable to assume it would have found its way into the earliest written account of Jesus's life. But Mark seems completely unaware of—or at least uninterested in—the virgin birth story. Mark presents his Gospel without the Jewish account of the birth of Jesus and without any reference to Jesus's Jewish genealogy. In contrast, all four Gospels give an account of the death and resurrection of Jesus. Perhaps Mark simply cared more about the adult life and ministry of Jesus and wanted to get right down to business. Either way, it's a striking omission from the earliest written record of Jesus's life.

Furthermore, Mark's Gospel suggests there was ambivalence about Jesus's identity, even among those closest to him. The disciples don't arrive at a full understanding of who Jesus really is or recognize his glory as divine Son of God until after Jesus dies. Jesus's own mother and brothers seem bewildered and confused by his actions at times (Mark 3:21–35). Jesus's return to his hometown elicits scorn and rejection; they referred to him as "the son of Mary" (Mark 6:3), which may have been an insulting reference to an illicit conception. Matthew's Gospel names Jesus as the child of both Joseph and Mary: "Is not this [Jesus] the carpenter's son? Is not his mother called Mary?" (Matthew 13:55). To his hometown folk, Jesus was just an average Joe. Some of his siblings still lived in the town. They were skeptical about this purported miracle-man and "took offense at him" (Mark 6:3; cf. Matthew 13:57).

The disciples catch glimpses of understanding here and there about Jesus's identity, such as the exclamation by Peter that Jesus is the "Christ . . . the Son of God" (Mark 8:27–30). And then, after Jesus's death on the cross, a witness cries out, "Truly this was God's Son" (Mark 15:39; cf. Matthew 27:54). But while Mark presents Jesus as the Messiah and the

Son of God (Mark 1:1), he also shows how Jesus's identity as divine was largely hidden throughout his life and only understood in pieces. Complete understanding awaited his death and resurrection.

Here's a big problem: If Mark and the early sources knew of a miraculous virgin birth of Jesus, some evidence of that knowledge should appear in the earliest Gospel. If Jesus was the product of a supernatural virgin birth, we'd expect the disciples to know about it, and we'd expect Mark to depict it or at least acknowledge it. But not only is the virgin birth story absent, Jesus's conception appears tinged by scandal.

The omission of the virgin birth story in Mark (and John) doesn't prove anything because it's an "argument from silence." Nonetheless, it's an important piece of a larger cumulative case, discouraging us from confidence in the historicity of the virgin birth stories. If nothing else, the conspicuous absence of the virgin birth throughout most of the New Testament suggests that what we believe about the beginning of Jesus's life isn't nearly as crucial as what we believe about the end of it. The earliest church tradition doesn't include the virgin birth; it only includes Jesus's death, burial, and resurrection: "For I handed on to you as of first importance what I in turn had received: that Christ died for our sins in accordance with the scriptures, and that he was buried, and that he was raised on the third day in accordance with the scriptures . . ." (1 Corinthians 15:3–4).

BUT WHAT ABOUT PAUL?

There's another glaring problem: the apostle Paul seems entirely unaware of the virgin birth. Paul's letters are chronologically the earliest writings in the New Testament. Seven of his letters were written between 50 and 60 CE, well before both the Gospels of Matthew and Luke. None of the letters attributed to Paul reference the virgin birth, nor do they reference Mary by name. Since they are the earliest New Testament writings, this is a conspicuous absence, indeed. You would think a remarkable story such as this would have spread quickly and broadly, at least within the early Christian communities.

While Paul doesn't mention anything remotely akin to a virgin birth, he does include a few references to Jesus's human origin. In Romans 1:3, he says that Jesus was born "of the seed of David according to the flesh." The term "seed" (*spermatos*) references male parentage; Jesus's royal lineage came through procreation via the seed (semen) of his father. The NIV translation omits "seed" from its translation of

Romans 1:3. Instead, it has "who was descended from David according to the flesh." This may reflect an uneasiness of the theologically conservative translation with the troubling implications of "seed" for the traditional doctrine of the virgin birth. Paul seems to assume that Jesus came from normal male-female procreation. You might even say that Jesus's royal Messianic status, as one of King David's progeny, depended on it.

In Galatians, we encounter the second reference to Jesus's human origins in Paul's writings. The same word for "seed" is used; this time it carries the sense of "offspring" or "child" (Galatians 3:16, 19). Paul names Christ as the seed (offspring) of Abraham. He presses the point that God fulfilled his promises to Abraham through his offspring, Jesus the Messiah.

At first glance, a third reference in Paul's letters appears to support a virginal conception. In Galatians 4:4–5, Paul writes that "God sent forth His Son," and then uses the phrase, "born of a woman." But this phrase doesn't indicate that Jesus was born *only* of a woman and not of a man. By "born of a woman," Paul insists that Jesus was really and truly human. In other words, he was born from a woman's womb, like everyone else. He wasn't miraculously dropped out of the sky or created out of thin air. For

Paul, Jesus wasn't a phantom, but the Son of God as a true human being.

A fourth reference occurs in 2 Timothy 2:8, which includes the phrase "a descendant of David" to denote the Messianic status of Jesus Christ. Many scholars doubt that Paul wrote this letter; nonetheless, the reference only further confirms the importance of Joseph as Jesus's biological father.

And that's it. Paul's letters include a total of three—possibly four—references to Jesus's human origins, none of which hint at a virginal conception. So, Paul was either unaware of the virgin birth or he didn't consider it important enough to write about, even though he was developing a Christ-centered and thoroughly incarnational theology. Paul alludes to Christ's preexistence status in Philippians 2:6–11, when he quotes an early hymn that proclaims the glory of Christ's incarnation as a human being and his exaltation at the resurrection. Christ existed "in the form of God" prior to the incarnation and even prior to creation itself (Philippians 2:6). That's what caught Paul's attention: The preexistent divine logos, the cosmic Christ, and the resurrected Lord. But no virgin birth.

By itself, the lack of reference by Paul to a virgin birth doesn't constitute proof either for or against its historicity; there were surely a number of things

Paul knew and believed about Jesus that he didn't include in his letters. But Paul consistently exalts the supremacy of Christ and affirms the centrality of the incarnation. Given his "high Christology," one would expect Paul to use the virgin birth to drive home the uniqueness of Jesus and his divine origin, particularly in a context where important figures were often associated with miraculous origins. But he didn't, maybe because he understood that a theology of incarnation doesn't depend on a supernatural conception. But more likely, Paul didn't know the virgin birth stories and had no reason to see any conflict between his exalted view of Christ and Jesus's fully human conception.

If Jesus's birth had been an ordinary biological conception between Joseph and Mary as a married couple or a scandalous one (either premarital sex or rape), we would expect to see exactly what we see in Paul's writings: a few vague references to Jesus being born "of a woman" (a normal, human birth), a natural-born Messiah from "Abraham's seed," and a descendant of David "according to the flesh." Also, the Christ and Lord of all.

We've arrived at a pivotal moment. Upon examination of the biblical evidence, a case has been building, and the pressure mounting. But there's more to consider.

A CONFLICTED PRESENCE

Matthew and Luke are the two most important sources for the traditional Christian belief in the virgin birth. Their infancy narratives share several narrative elements. They both include genealogies that verify Jesus's royal, Davidic, Messianic credentials. In both, Jesus is born of the virgin Mary through the Holy Spirit (not by human sexual intercourse), and Joseph is her husband. Both include the appearance of a divine messenger who proclaims the baby's name will be Jesus. Both link Jesus's birth to the reign of King Herod. Both have Jesus being born in Bethlehem and raised in Nazareth.[2]

But the two Gospels also contain some striking differences as well as problematic details, both internally and in comparison to each other. The striking differences recall my daughter's tangled string and my son's snarled Slinkies.

In Matthew, an unnamed angel appears and speaks to Joseph, but not to Mary. In Luke, the angel, there named Gabriel, appears and speaks to Mary, but not to Joseph. In Matthew, the family migrates to Egypt following the visit of the Magi to escape Herod's violent wrath (Matthew 2:13–14). In Luke's account, shepherds, rather than the Magi, come to visit Jesus in Bethlehem after being notified by angels. In Luke, Mary and Joseph bring the newborn Jesus home to Nazareth in Galilee, following his circumcision ritual in the temple (Luke 2:39–40), with no reference to a flight to Egypt or to a conflict with Herod.

Both Matthew and Luke set Jesus's birth in Bethlehem, linking the event to biblical prophecy (Matthew 2:6; cf. Micah 5:2). Matthew places Jesus's birth in Bethlehem in fulfillment of the prophecy, whereas Luke positions Jesus's birth in Bethlehem because of a Roman census (Luke 2:1–7). In Matthew's account, Joseph and Mary were already living in Bethlehem when the divine conception, the angel's announcement, and the birth took place. In Luke, Mary and Joseph were living in Nazareth when the divine announcement and pregnancy happened, and they only traveled to Bethlehem because of the census and Joseph's royal Davidic lineage.

In Luke, the family returns to their home in Nazareth from Bethlehem following the birth, census, and ritual dedication of Jesus. But in Matthew the family flees to Egypt from their home in Bethlehem to escape from King Herod. In Matthew, Jesus is nearly two years old when the escape to Egypt occurs, whereas in Luke, the family "returned peaceably to Nazareth after the birth at Bethlehem."[3] We should also note that the two genealogies include notable differences when compared alongside each other. For one striking example, Luke lists Joseph's father as Heli (Luke 3:23), while Matthew says his name is Jacob (Matthew 1:16).

What a tangled web they weave!

And what kind of manger scene is this? A complicated one, to say the least. And a conflicted one, too.

There are also problems with historical details within the individual accounts themselves. Consider Luke's account of the census. The timing of the census, with Quirinius the governor of Syria and Augustus the emperor, conflicts chronologically with the information given earlier in Luke about Herod's reign as king of Judea. Quirinius did not become governor of Syria until 6 CE, and he remained as governor until 12 CE. It's well established that King Herod died in 4 BCE.[4] So Quirinius was not governor of Syria while Herod was king over Judea—that's simply a mistake. Furthermore, if John the Baptist and Jesus were both born in the last year of Herod's life, as Luke indicates, that would make Jesus no less than ten years old and perhaps even sixteen years old at the time of the census and—consequently, according to Luke's narration—at the time of his own birth (as described in Luke 2:1–7).[5] Unless some serious time travel was going on, this is another error.

The presence of these narrative contradictions and historical problems doesn't necessarily invalidate the traditional view of the virgin birth. If issues like these disqualified a biblical story, we'd have to toss out the resurrection, too, because the four resurrection accounts conflict with each other on several details. For that matter, we'd probably have to discount the whole life and ministry of Jesus. Frankly, from the perspective of modern record-keeping, most of ancient history is sketchy. But we shouldn't hold ancient writers to the accuracy standards of contemporary journalistic reporting or historical biography.

On this logic, we shouldn't jump to conclusions too hastily. But if the weight of an argument tilts strongly in one direction, it's intellectually responsible to let the evidence shape one's position. But intellectual humility is required on the other side of the conclusion, too. There's no time machine to take us back into first-century Judea and Galilee to finally prove the case one way or another. On historical matters, certainty eludes us.

ISAIAH'S YOUNG WOMAN AND MATTHEW'S VIRGIN

I worked as a youth pastor for two years while I was in seminary. Some of the Bible study curriculum published by the denomination just blew my mind—and not in a good way. Soon after I began working at the church, I pulled out a Bible study lesson on prophecy, thinking it could make for an intriguing Wednesday-night youth group discussion. The lesson included an assignment asking students to form small groups and look up about fifty Bible verses, matching an Old Testament prophecy with its "fulfillment" in the New Testament. Students had the hardest time figuring out how, exactly, the New Testament verses had anything to do with the Old Testament prophecy. And as I worked along with the confused students, I was flummoxed, too. The author found "fulfillments" of prophecy under every biblical rock, thereby demonstrating the truth of the Bible.

In seminary, I learned that Hebrew prophecy didn't typically have anything to do with predictions about the future that would eventually come true (à la Nostradamus). Instead, prophecy was typically a hard word from God for the people of God: a stern warning that if they didn't change their ways to align with righteousness and justice, they would feel the consequences. I was proud of my youth group for seeing the assignment for what it was: a desperate overreach, with no real textual basis.

I used to believe that the virgin birth story was supported by Old Testament prophecy. Matthew 1:23 includes a reference to Isaiah 7:14:

Look, the virgin shall conceive and bear a son,
and they shall name him Emmanuel.

But in Isaiah, neither Jesus of Nazareth nor the "Virgin Mary" are anywhere to be found.

(Take a deep breath—we're going to do a brief language study here.)

The Hebrew word for "virgin" doesn't appear in the original Hebrew text of Isaiah 7:14. The original Hebrew text uses 'almah, which is normally translated "young woman," though it can have the meaning, "young woman of marriageable age." But Matthew was quoting the Septuagint, an early Greek translation of the original Hebrew Old Testament. The Septuagint used the Greek term *parthenos* in Isaiah 7:14 in place of 'almah to mean young woman. *Parthenos* can also mean virgin, but it doesn't always, and that certainly wasn't the most accurate rendering in this case. Nonetheless, the Septuagint translation provided Matthew with a handy tool for his purposes: linking the birth of Jesus to an Old Testament prophetic text.

Got that?

But apart from Matthew's creative theological rendering, the Old Testament lends no direct support to the traditional view of the virgin birth. Matthew's use of the prophecy from Isaiah enhances his narrative of Jesus's birth by linking Jesus to the ancient Hebrew anticipation of and longing for the salvation of Israel. This is not unusual or even wrong; New Testament authors commonly took creative license with Old Testament texts. But there's an unavoidable implication: The Bible is not inerrant. God didn't supernaturally protect the Bible and its authors from errors, whether those errors pertain to history or science. This is no less true of the Gospels themselves. While the Gospels give us the story of God working through Jesus, they do so through the lenses of a different time and place, and through the lenses of a new theological orientation.

IF THE VIRGIN BIRTH DIDN'T HAPPEN, THEN THE BIBLE ISN'T INERRANT (AND THAT'S OKAY)

One of my professors at the conservative evangelical college I attended shook my faith to the core—but not in the way you're thinking. At the end of a class session I asked the professor what I considered to be a legitimate and probably sophomoric question (but hey, I was a sophomore). The professor lectured on Genesis 4, the story of Cain's murder of his brother, Abel. God punished Cain, expelling him as a "fugitive and wanderer" on the earth. A distraught Cain complained to the Lord that "anyone who meets me may kill me" (Genesis 4:14). God's response was a merciful one: He would put a mark on Cain that signified that whoever hurt Cain would be subject to mortal punishment (Genesis 4:15).

I asked my professor, "If Adam and Eve were the first two humans created, and if Cain and Abel were their first children, where in the world did all these other people come from that Cain was so worried about? How did they get there? Incest and rapid procreation? That seems unlikely."

He looked at me as if I had just kicked his dog. He looked me dead in the eye, as if he was either about to cry or report me to the dean, and said, "Are you trying to make me question my faith?" And then he walked off.

On that day, I learned that some questions are too much for some people. On the positive side, I discovered that even highly accomplished Christian professors have weaknesses in their faith. My professor was probably dealing with anxieties about his theology—and perhaps his vocation, too. But it struck me as deeply problematic that a question as basic as "where did all these other people come from?" was ruled out-of-bounds. My professor chastised me for asking critical questions of the Bible, our sacred authority.

The evangelical preoccupation with the doctrine of inerrancy—that the Bible is without error in any respect, including history, geography, and science—reflects an anxiety about the legitimacy of their theological beliefs and, derivatively, of the institutions grounded on those beliefs. Inerrancy functions like a buffer against uncertainty or ambiguity. It's a stop sign, a warning against asking too many questions. Inerrancy throws up a roadblock and says, "Go no further!" As a result, like the professor who rebuffed my question, it leaves many honest questioners in the dark, with nowhere to go, made to feel disruptive or disrespectful when they seek to go deeper, to push beyond the developmental wall of critical questioning, into a more open, rich, and meaningful faith.[6] Finding no opening or welcome, many honest doubters just walk away.

Even the staunchest proponents of the historicity of the virgin birth must admit that it's at least a bit unsettling that, outside of Matthew and Luke, none of the rest of the New Testament makes any explicit mention of the virgin birth. References to Jesus's human origin are few and far between. The conflicts and problems with the differing details in the two Gospel accounts suggest that the reader should feel freedom in approaching the infancy narratives other than as straightforward histories, literally true in every detail.

As I see it, the problems in the infancy narratives create an opportunity. We need not be despondent about what this means for our faith. Rather, we can explore new ways of reading these narratives and of understanding Jesus and the meaning of the incarnation for us today.

I considered myself to be an evangelical Christian for the better part of my life, up until several years ago. Since then, I've rejected the doctrine of inerrancy, a doctrine that reveals an unnecessary and problematic anxiety about the certainty of our faith and beliefs. For many years now I've read the

Genesis creation story as mythic in its shape and theological in its intention: the real takeaway is neither historical nor scientific. Similarly, I've learned to read Jonah not as a historically true story about a man being swallowed whole by a fish, but as a parable or satire, teaching a lesson about grace, judgmental attitudes, and God's inclusion of all people in salvation. I learned to read the Old Testament stories of God sanctioning violence and commanding genocide as religious propaganda that reflected more the hostile environment of the Ancient Near East than the character of the true God of Israel, who is revealed most clearly and definitively in Jesus Christ.[7]

And now I can approach the virgin birth stories, also, through the lens of reflective, faithful questioning.

The Bible is not only a divine book, inspired by the Holy Spirit and given for our edification and salvation, but also a human book, mirroring the influences of the original cultures and worldviews, and reflecting the literary forms and theological intentions of its authors.

The virgin birth stories come to us in aesthetically effective and theologically rich narratives that have clearly captivated Christian imagination for centuries. But like Genesis, Jonah, and the genocide in Joshua, these stories should be read in the context of the broader witness of Scripture, recognizing that biblical stories and theological traditions develop over time in ever-changing contexts, and all the while engaging contemporary scientific knowledge in our interpretations.

We've come a long way on our journey, now. I've got a sense that moving beyond traditional belief in the virgin birth could open new pathways, at once more divine and more human. Thanks to faithful questioning.

FROM THE ASHES OF DECONSTRUCTION, NEW LIFE COMES

In seminary faculty lounges across the country, professors debate a perennial subject: Do they expend too much effort in deconstructing their students' beliefs, without providing them enough building blocks for reconstruction? This discussion was especially common at the evangelical seminary where I taught for nearly a decade. Invariably, the most conservative faculty would charge the most progressive faculty with doing too much deconstruction in our classrooms, and not enough reconstruction. (Some of them really meant *indoctrination*.)

One day the discussion spilled over into my classroom, and I began having this discussion directly with students. Adam, a bright and theologically progressive student, observed that what's *deconstructive* for some students can be very *reconstructive* and life-giving for others. Some students feel threatened by the introduction of new intellectual and theological questions. But for others—like Adam—their faith languishes because the picture of God they've inherited is too boxed-in and the theology they've imbibed is too rigid for an honest and authentic faith. That discussion helped shift the way I think about the role of theological education and how educators raise difficult questions with students.

I recall a friend who, upon hearing that I was working on this book, exclaimed with worry: "But why fiddle with a foundational doctrine like the virgin birth? What could it mean for your faith? What might it do to the faith of your readers?" From the beginning, my hope has been that this journey would deepen faith, not weaken it. From the rubble of deconstruction, new life can emerge.

It's time to answer the question: Was Jesus born of a virgin, or not?

The biblical and historical evidence points us away from the traditional view of the virgin birth, suggesting the infancy narratives were legends that were added to the earlier and more widely attested testimonies to Jesus's death and resurrection. This strand of evidence is added to arguments from contemporary science, which renders problematic a human virginal conception—a "divine artificial insemination." On top of all that, we've faced the most vexing problem of all: the logic of the incarnation conflicts with the notion of a virginal conception. If God really became a human being, then he was born not just of a woman, but of a man, too. This "cumulative case" should motivate us to consider the human origins of the divine Son of God through another lens.

The deconstruction has been done. We can move beyond the traditional view of the virgin birth. But if you're looking at me like my professor did—like I just kicked your dog!—let me assure you: The story that emerges from the rubble of deconstruction is more interesting and even more inspiring than the traditional one.

Along with the deafening silence of the rest of the New Testament and the presence of contradictions and complications both within and across the two Gospel accounts, hints of an alternative narrative appear: Jesus's birth wasn't a miraculous, virginal conception, but an ordinary birth. But amid the ordinary, something extraordinary happens.

I still read the infancy narratives as a reminder that, in the hands of God, the future is not closed. The stories draw attention to the central Christian belief that Jesus Christ is the Son of God, the Messiah, and the unique manifestation of God within the vagaries of history. They underscore the role of Jesus in God's salvation history. The virgin birth heightened the beginning of the Jesus story, so that it matched the climax—the resurrection—in narrative power and supernatural intensity.

But to appreciate these narrative insights, we don't need to read them literally as straightforward, factual-in-every-way histories. By moving beyond a literal virgin birth, we can recover a complete incarnation of the Son of God, through human procreation. God invites all people to participate in redemption. But God becomes one of us in the personhood of Jesus of Nazareth, too. Right here, with us as Emmanuel.

NOTES

1. Raymond Brown, *Birth of the Messiah: A Commentary on the Infancy Narratives in the Gospels of Matthew and Luke* (New Haven: Yale University Press, 1999), 27.

2. Ibid., 34–35.

3. Ibid., 36.

4. The ancient historian Josephus recorded that Herod's death occurred the night before a lunar eclipse, which occurred on March 12 or 13, in 4 BCE.

5. See Andrew Lincoln, *Born of a Virgin? Reconceiving Jesus in the Bible, Tradition, and Theology* (Grand Rapids, MI: Eerdmans, 2013), 139–42.

6. See James Fowler, *Stages of Faith: The Psychology of Human Development and the Quest for Meaning* (New York: HarperCollins, 1995), and Robert Guelich and Janet Hagberg, *The Critical Journey: Stages in the Life of Faith*, 2nd edition (Salem, WI: Sheffield, 2005).

7. See Kenneth Sparks, *God's Word in Human Words: An Evangelical Appropriation of Critical Biblical Scholarship* (Grand Rapids, MI: Baker Academic, 2008).

6

HOW NOT TO LOSE YOUR BABY JESUS

"Just bring the baby Jesus back. Just put him back there, and everyone would be happy."

With those words, Barbara Shearer pleaded to the anonymous thief who stole the baby Jesus from her church's outdoor nativity scene in Burlington, Wisconsin. The prank left Mary and Joseph staring blankly into a manger filled with hay, but no baby.[1]

"I looked in there and I said, 'the baby Jesus is gone!'"

Shearer's exasperation illustrates the frustration many people feel when you mess with their manger scene.

I'm not a thief. I'm not a prankster. I haven't

taken the baby Jesus away. To the contrary, I want to put a *fully human* Jesus back into the nativity, back into the story of the human life of the divine Son of God.

This is serious and tricky business.

When I presented the problems with the Bible's virgin birth accounts to a church study group, one man argued: "Since no other source tells us how Jesus was conceived, isn't it better to simply rely on the biblical accounts that we do have? Isn't it safer to simply trust the infancy narratives of Matthew and Luke?"

It's a fair question.

For some, the best response to uncertainty about "what really happened" is to read the two Gospel accounts literally, as if they offer factual reports of a historical event. But that would require overlooking strong evidence to the contrary. Even if the authors of the Gospels believed they were relaying perfectly accurate histories of the origin of Jesus—and we can't say that for sure—that wouldn't obligate us to share their assumptions. (Let's be honest: There are a *lot* of assumptions we don't share with the ancient authors of Scripture!) This gives us breathing room to ask faithful questions, bringing contemporary perspectives and knowledge to bear on our interpretations of the sacred text.

I hope that church in Wisconsin got their baby Jesus back.

My manger scene still has the baby Jesus; he didn't leave when the virgin birth disappeared. We can move beyond belief in the traditional view of the virgin birth, and still be faithful followers of Jesus. But we're faced with the question of what replaces the virginal conception. How was Jesus conceived, if not by a miraculous act of the Holy Spirit in a virgin mother?

There is no way to confidently recover the *real* story behind the conception of Jesus. We simply lack the historical material to give a definitive answer. But we can imagine two broad, hypothetical scenarios.

OPTION A: EXTRAORDINARY PEOPLE HAVE REMARKABLE BIRTHS

Of the available hypothetical scenarios, the least controversial theory is that Mary and Joseph had sexual intercourse within marriage, resulting in the conception of Jesus. On this scenario, the infancy narratives were legends that emerged in the context of the early Jewish-Christian Jesus communities. The stories may have developed in response to the common intuition that an ordinary birth didn't suffice for someone of the Messiah's stature. Legendary or mythic stories for important figures were common in the ancient world, because a remarkable person needs a compelling origin story.

My son, Luke, loves superheroes and science fiction stories. When Sara and I decided on his name, I knew that one day I would have the privilege of role-playing Star Wars with him, and uttering some of the most famous words in cinematic history: "Luke, I am your father!" And recently, I dressed in black, put a black fire engine hat over my face, and dueled my Luke Skywalker son, chasing him with a dollar-store light saber around the family room.

Generations of fans admire the mythology of the Star Wars films and books. George Lucas was influenced by Joseph Campbell, and Campbell taught that myths generate shared meaning and a common cultural and moral framework for a society. Myths commonly include heroes: transcendent, larger-than-life figures (often gods) who have equally larger-than-life origins. Peruse the hero stories and films in our own culture and you'll see that good myths include powerful origin stories.

Christians often assume that Jesus's virgin birth makes him unique among important religious figures, perhaps even proving his divinity. But many ancient mythologies included stories about gods procreating with female humans. A miraculous origin story involving divine intervention shows that the heroic figure is unique and worthy of devotion. Among other ancient cultures, Greco-Roman and Egyptian literature includes numerous accounts of divine-human births including some highly unusual conceptions—though none of them are exact parallels to the Gospels' virgin birth stories.[2] The Egyptian god Horus was conceived when his mother, the goddess Isis, pieced back together the dismembered body of her dead husband, the god Osiris. Since she couldn't retrieve Osiris's phallus (it'd been eaten by a catfish in the Nile), she made one of gold instead—the gold replacement apparently did the trick. For an example from the Greco-Roman side, Alexander the Great was rumored to have been conceived when Zeus struck the womb of Olympia, Alexander's mother, with a lightning bolt. Talk about starting life with a bang.

That's just the tip of the miracle-birth iceberg in the ancient world.

Structural similarities between the Gospels' infancy narratives and other ancient legendary stories of important figures place them within the genre "ancient biography," which commonly included legendary motifs.[3] Andrew Lincoln finds several themes in common between Matthew/Luke and ancient mythologies, including angelic announcements, dreams, predictions of a future savior, babies leaping in the womb (with accompanying explanations), and attempts to prevent male children from being born, among others.[4] But other ancient accounts differ in many respects from the Gospels, especially regarding the manner of impregnation by the divine figure. Nonbiblical stories often included more vivid and even lurid detail (like gold phalluses and lightning bolts). The Gospels are subdued by comparison, lacking explicit reference to sexual activity between a god and a human.

While Matthew and Luke reveal similarities in style and content with some Greco-Roman and Egyptian stories, the biblical infancy narratives probably didn't heavily depend on any of them. But they do show the influence of sources that the Gospel's authors—and their readers—knew well: Hebrew stories of God's involvement in births of important figures, none of which include virginal conceptions.[5] God's protection of the baby Moses was a supernatural intervention, even though God wasn't directly involved in his conception. God miraculously enabled Sarah, the wife of Abraham, to give birth to Isaac at an extremely advanced age. God answered Hannah's prayers, healing her barren womb and allowing the prophet Samuel to come into the world. These Hebrew stories differed from the virginal conception stories in that they involved two human parents, male and female. Nonetheless, the stories indicate the strong hand of God's providence, either in conception and birth, or through protection from harm at an early age.

The virgin birth stories may have emerged organically and naturally as Jesus's fame spread through the early Christian communities. The faithful told stories about their hero, their Lord, their Messiah, their divine Son of God. In this scenario, the authors of Matthew and Luke weren't being deceptive by including these stories. They used communication devices and themes common to the ancient world, shaping their biographies to make theological points.

OPTION B: A SCANDALOUS PREGNANCY

There's another possible scenario: perhaps a scandalous event lay behind the human origin of Jesus. A scandal, whether rape or consensual, premarital sex, could have led to a cover-up: an alternative story about Jesus's birth within the faithful and growing community of his followers. Perhaps Mary and Joseph simply had sexual relations prior to the legal ratification of their marriage, thereby breaking strict Jewish law. The virgin birth stories could have emerged as a kind of "apologetic" (defensive) response to awareness of an illicit conception.

In the early days of Christianity, skeptics levied all sorts of arguments against it. Defenders of Christianity took them on, asserting the credibility of the Christian religion and the legitimacy of Jesus as its centerpiece. The theologian Origen wrote an early apologetic essay in which he defended the virginal conception of Jesus and the integrity of Jesus's origin. He disputed the claims of Celsus, a pagan philosopher and opponent of Christianity, who had argued that the virgin birth story was a fiction invented by Jesus himself due to embarrassment about the truth of his scandalous birth.[6] Celsus held that Jesus was the biological product of his mother and a Roman soldier named Panthera. The soldier impregnated Mary, who then gave birth to Jesus alone and in secret—because she had been spurned by Joseph for her "adultery."[7] Origen's recounting doesn't clearly specify whether the rumor involved rape or consensual adultery; but in the ancient world, soldiers were known to commit violent sexual acts against vulnerable persons.

The Gospels imply the presence of rumors of an illicit conception of Jesus. Mark includes a rather provocative story about Jesus returning to his hometown and getting some pretty rude treatment. In Mark 6:1–6, the people of Jesus's hometown, skeptical of his miracles and questioning his teachings, ask a potentially revealing question: "Is this not the carpenter, the *son of Mary*, and brother of James?" Some scholars suggest that the phrase, "son of Mary," isn't a reference to Mary as sole parent of Jesus; rather, it may have been a "bitter insult," a rude reference to Jesus's illegitimate conception.[8] In effect, they might have been calling Jesus a bastard (a *mamzer*, from the Hebrew).

The expected reference would have been "son of Joseph," since the father establishes the pedigree. This is exactly the designation used in the parallel accounts in Matthew and Luke. Mark, contra those two later Gospels, may have included this bitter, rude insult either out of brashness or out of naïveté. Perhaps the only story Mark knew about Jesus's birth involved an "illegitimate" pregnancy: whether via consensual-but-illegal sexual relations (against Jewish moral law) or through sexual violence.

But there's an alternative explanation for Mark's use of the phrase "son of Mary." It's possible that Mark isn't referring to an illicit conception at all; if Joseph had several wives over time (as early Christian tradition attests—remember our significantly older Joseph!), the phrase might have been used to distinguish Jesus as the child of *Mary*—rather than Joseph's other or former wife.[9]

James McGrath argues that, based on the adult Jesus's social interactions, Jesus probably wasn't the product of an illegitimate conception.[10] For one thing, if he were a "mamzer" (bastard) and consequently bore the social stigma of illegitimacy, his willingness to fraternize with people from the lower castes would have elicited no surprise or consternation. But he was often criticized by Pharisees and other religious elites for doing just that. They took Jesus to task for stooping to the level of the socially marginalized, which suggests that they considered Jesus to be of respectable status:

In effect: "Jesus, what are you thinking, hanging out with that riff-raff?"

Nonetheless, if Jesus was "illegitimate"—or if he were merely tainted as such—this scandal would have given detractors fuel for their fire. From a modern, Western perspective, it seems strange that an episode as mundane as premarital sex could motivate a story of a miraculous pregnancy. But in the Hebrew context of the first century—as is still the case in some non-Western societies—premarital sex and adultery were punishable by death. This harsh legalistic reality lies behind Matthew's explanation of Joseph's intention: "Her husband Joseph, being a righteous man and unwilling to expose her to public disgrace, planned to dismiss her quietly" (Matthew 1:19). Both Jews and Christians would have had difficulty accepting rape as the historical origin of their Messiah, and this would have cast a negative light on Jesus as an important religious figure within the framework of the first century.

While any certainty about this question eludes us, it's possible that a virgin birth story emerged to counter rumors of Jesus's illegitimate conception.

The early presence of a rumor does not, in and of itself, disprove the historicity of the virgin birth. There would have been compelling political reasons for some early Jews and Romans to try to discredit Jesus's uniqueness, just as there would have been political reasons for defending it. Everybody has a bias; everybody has a motive; everybody has a story.

But it's also impossible to prove the contrary: that the rumors were falsehoods perpetuated by people trying to undermine belief in Jesus.

I'm most drawn to *Option A*, the least controversial and most natural theory: that Mary and Joseph, a newly married couple, had consensual sexual intercourse, leading to the conception of Jesus. If a consensual sexual union led to the conception of Jesus (whether pre- or within marriage matters little for this point), this affirms in a basic and beautiful way the goodness of creation and of human procreation. But if the sexual act was violent and coercive, then the conception of Jesus shows us that, from the very beginning of his story, the incarnation means that God redeems the evil of the world—evils that even his own mother experienced—from inside its brokenness.

None of these scenarios, if true, would detract from the key point of the Gospels and from the central message of Christianity: Jesus of Nazareth was and is the divine Son of God, Emmanuel, God-with-us. None would detract from or undermine the point of the gospel itself, which the apostle Paul proclaimed to be a scandal to Jews and a stumbling block to Gentiles.

To sum up: We can't recover the lost story of Jesus's conception. But it makes sense that the virgin birth stories were later additions to the already-circulating stories about Jesus's life, teachings, death, and resurrection. In the ancient world, important figures needed remarkable beginnings —and a Messiah, Son of God, and Savior certainly qualifies as an important figure. The stories may also have functioned as apologetic defenses of Jesus and Christianity against the rumor of an illicit conception. They certainly added a dramatic miracle to the beginning of what was already the remarkable life and miraculous ending of Jesus of Nazareth.

The logic of the incarnation traces all the way back to a human conception and makes the most sense without a supernatural virginal conception, or "divine artificial insemination." That we cannot confidently establish the factual story of the conception of Jesus doesn't erase that key point.

THE LEGEND OF THE VIRGIN BIRTH

After all the deconstruction is done and the smoke clears, it's important to reimagine how the infancy narratives of Matthew and Luke factor into our faith and our theology.

Many contemporary readers apply basic critical reflection to biblical texts to derive meaning and significance from them. When we read the creation stories of Genesis 1–3, many of us don't expect to acquire factually true, literal history; nor do we expect to find a valid scientific explanation for the origins of the universe and of human life. We may read the story of Jonah as figurative or illustrative, meant to teach a lesson about Israel's disobedience to God and their ethnic and religious superiority complex. Most Christians today read Paul's command that women should cover their heads during worship in church, "because of the angels" (1 Corinthians 11:10), as making a specifically local and contextual point from within his own worldview. We rightly assume we can read the Bible both faithfully and critically.

But the Gospels seem like a sacred exception, immune to critical inquiry. Taking account of the different worldviews of the original authors of the Gospels can make us anxious. It feels like playing on a different field than the creation stories, or giant man-swallowing fish, or Paul's strange statements about angels and head-coverings. The Gospels are about Jesus, not to be messed with! My long history within conservative Christianity has disposed me to read the Gospels with a default of trust, assuming historicity and a basic level of factuality. Digging beneath the surface of the stories has felt improper at times. "Don't mess with my manger scene!" Remember?

I've pushed through that default position and have come to conclude that the best way to think about the infancy narratives is as *legend*. Legends differ from myths, which are stories told and passed along within a culture that give meaning and significance to the human experience. Myths make sense out of the disparate, fractured elements of human and social life. In the broadest sense, myths address questions about human origins, meanings, and destiny.

Myths are more abstract than legends; they're more detached from history. Myths feature gods and goddesses, whereas legends are fanciful exaggerations of events and heroic but real-life figures that have some historical grounding. Legends take place in something akin to real places and times, in the "remembered past"—rather than in some primordial, timeless beginning or ethereal place, which is often the context of myths.[11]

The infancy narratives of Matthew and Luke fall in the category of legend, fitting somewhere between myths (abstracted from history, detached from reality) and realistic, factual narrative histories.[12] The stories are told against the backdrop of what appears to be real, historical time and place. Unlike myths, they are not primarily about God or gods; they tell about a human person, albeit a unique one. Of course, God is involved too, a point that blurs the stark division between myth and legend. But the larger point of the infancy stories is not the origin of a god, but the appearance of the Messiah (Christ) on the historical stage—the long-promised and now-arriving liberation of Israel and the arrival of God's kingdom.

The Christian church has long viewed the virgin

birth account as crucial to Christian theology and to an adequate understanding of Jesus Christ. We should respect the weight of tradition as well as the authority of Scripture, but we cannot let either tradition or Scripture crush faithful, critical questioning, or subdue the spirit of liberation. The truth of the legend of the birth of Jesus lies somewhere between the naïve assumption that everything happened exactly as described, and the skeptical refusal to believe that anything described took place.[13] Neither tradition nor dogma provides sufficient reason to insist on a literal reading of the infancy narratives.

But we should read them *literarily*, which is to say, as stories whose inclusion in the Gospel accounts framed the theology and meaning of the stories of Jesus. We can appreciate their narrative beauty, symbolic power, and theological meaning. The Gospels present distinct but complementary theological perspectives on Jesus of Nazareth, a person who represents God and God's liberation for Israel within the context of a messy, conflict-ridden world and who manifests divine love in our space and in our time. The Gospels culminate in the death of the Messiah and Son of God at the hands of religious and political authorities. The story ends not in tragedy, but in triumph. God resurrects Jesus in the power of the

Spirit, signaling God's eventual triumph over death, sin, and evil.

RENEWING HUMANITY, FROM WITHIN HUMANITY

In the Gospels, Jesus is the Messiah and divine Son of God whose dramatic entrance into history marks a pivotal moment in the history of Israel and in the redemption of the world. Mary is a significant participant in liberation; she's an assertive and faithful person whom God blesses with a key role within salvation history. Her virginity is not the point. Her sexuality is not the point. Her motherhood isn't even the point. The point is that, through the agency of Mary, and through the birth of Jesus in the power of the Spirit, something new arrived—a new way of being, a new way of living, a new world colliding with the present one.

God's grace has been uniquely and powerfully poured out in Jesus of Nazareth. Jesus is God's presence within and to our history. He marks the "descent" of the eternal God to our time and place. But Jesus also illustrates what humanity can become, inviting us to follow in the path he lays out before us. In and through Jesus, God opens new possibilities for humanity and for creation to live in accordance with love and grace, not hate and destruction. We should be careful, however, not to imply that a "new humanity" means an altogether different humanity. Yes, Jesus's human life differs from ours ("yet without sin"), but he is not different *in kind*. The incarnation means that God is truly human in Jesus of Nazareth.

God initiates the in-breaking of the new creation in the person of Jesus. The implications of this reach far beyond individual salvation or even inward spiritual renewal. They are political, economic, and liberating, stretching from the social world of first-century Judea, living in the context of imperial Roman rule, across the entirety of creation. A new age has dawned in Jesus. The birth of the Christ child opened a window to the future—the arrival of the great promise in the form of a vulnerable baby.

In the context and thought-structure of the ancient world, the virgin birth symbolized the dawning of that new age. But, in the developing witness of the entirety of the New Testament, that symbol paled in comparison to the resurrection of Jesus—depicted in vivid though at times contrasting color in each of the four Gospels. In the cross and the resurrection, the world has been shaken by the power of God to conquer death, sin, and evil.

That's how you can move beyond the traditional

belief in the virgin birth and not lose the baby Jesus. Something happened; something new, something powerful, something remarkable, but something surprisingly human. The Easter resurrection moment begins with the Christmas nativity, with the conception and birth of Christ. The dusty and conflict-ridden world of the peasant girl, who gave birth in pain and in joy, with water and with blood. The human body, blood, bone, brain, and DNA of the divine Son of God.

Moving beyond the virgin birth allows us to embrace the idea that when the Son of God became incarnate as Jesus Christ, he entered the world in the most typical of ways: through human procreation. Perhaps Jesus was born not just through divine love, but human love, too—the love of a mother and of a father, for their child and for each other. Human sexual intercourse, giving birth to the divine Son of God as Jesus of Nazareth.

There's not much I can say for certain, but this I believe and confess: The divine Son of God became a true human being.

Notes

1. http://fox6now.com/2016/01/07/church-officials-in-burlington-plead-for-stolen-nativity-statues-return-just-bring-baby-jesus-back/.

2. Thomas Boslooper, *The Virgin Birth* (Philadelphia: Westminster, 1962), 136.

3. Andrew Lincoln, *Born of a Virgin? Reconceiving Jesus in the Bible, Tradition, and Theology* (Grand Rapids, MI: Eerdmans, 2013), 66.

4. Ibid., 62.

5. Raymond Brown, *The Virginal Conception and Bodily Resurrection of Jesus* (Mahwah, NJ: Paulist), 63.

6. Origen, *Against Celsus*, in Alexander Roberts and James Donaldson, *Ante-Nicene Fathers*, 10 vols. (Buffalo, NY: Christian Literature, 1885–1896; Reprint, Grand Rapids, MI: Eerdmans, 1951–1956; Reprint, Peabody, MA: Hendrickson, 1994), vol. 4, 1.32.410ff.

7. Origen, *Against Celsus*, in Roberts and Donaldson, *Ante-Nicene Fathers*, vol. 4, 1.32.410.

8. Gerd Lüdemann, *Virgin Birth? The Real Story of Mary and Her Son Jesus*, trans. John Bowden (Harrisburg, PA: Trinity, 1998), 54; Jane Schaberg, *The Illegitimacy of Jesus:*

A *Feminist Theological Interpretation of the Infancy Narratives* (San Francisco: Harper & Row, 1987), 160–63.

9. Lincoln, *Born of a Virgin?*, 149–60. The "multiple wives" possibility was attested as early as the *Gospel of James* and by Epiphanus.

10. James McGrath, "Was Jesus Illegitimate? The Evidence of His Social Interactions," *Journal for the Study of the Historical Jesus* 5, no. 1 (2007): 81–100.

11. Richard Horsley, *The Liberation of Christmas: The Infancy Narratives in Social Context* (New York: Continuum, 1993), 12.

12. Horsley, *Liberation*, 17.

13. Eric Seibert says, "The truth lies somewhere in between those extremes and varies from text to text. Answering the historical question must be done on a case-by-case basis." Seibert, *Disturbing Divine Behavior: Troubling Old Testament Images of God* (Minneapolis: Fortress Press, 2009), 112. Note that Seibert, an Old Testament scholar, is referring to texts from the Hebrew Bible, though the same point applies to all biblical texts.

7

GOD'S DEEP DIVE
INTO CREATION

One recent Sunday, I stood in our church's sun-
soaked sanctuary and recited the Apostles' Creed,
right along with the rest of the congregation:

> I believe in God, the Father almighty,
> creator of heaven and earth.
> I believe in Jesus Christ, God's only Son, our Lord,
> who was conceived by the Holy Spirit,
> born of the Virgin Mary . . .

I had spoken these words so many times before. But
this time, the phrases, "conceived by the Holy
Spirit" and "born of the Virgin Mary," hit me like a
blunt object.

Not much time had passed since my theological

shift when I stood in church and said that ancient creed. So much history lay behind those words. So much theological debate. So many developments. And so many problems. I was saying the words, but softly. As I repeated them, I thought about how my beliefs had changed.

For so much of my life, the virgin birth formed a piece of my core beliefs. Now I had to come to grips with the fact that I stood outside of the majority Christian tradition on this fundamental doctrine. But I'm not alone.

On December 4, 2016, Andy Stanley preached a controversial sermon. Referring to the virgin birth, he said,

> *A lot of people just don't believe it. And I understand that.... You've heard me say some version of this a million times, so this will be old if you've been around for a while. But see, if somebody can predict their own death and then their own resurrection, I'm not all that concerned about how they got into the world.*[1]

And then the pastor dropped the bomb:

Christianity doesn't hinge on the truth or even the stories around the birth of Jesus. It hinges on the resurrection of Jesus.[2]

Stanley clarified in follow-up sermons that he personally affirms the traditional belief in the virgin birth. The purpose of his controversial comment, he noted, was to create some intellectual breathing room for honest doubters. Christians can struggle with doctrines like the virgin birth and consider themselves faithful followers of Christ. The pastor also communicated a point accepted by many Christian theologians today: the virgin birth doesn't anchor Christian faith and hope; that job goes to the incarnation and resurrection.

Stanley's sermon drew the ire of some conservative, doctrinal gatekeepers. They worry that giving room for skepticism about the historicity of the virgin birth creates a slippery slope to apostasy. Give an inch, they'll take a mile—they say. For fundamentalists, if you reject the virgin birth you lose the incarnation and the divinity of Christ. If you lose the incarnation and the divinity of Christ, you've got no resurrection, either. And you can kiss your salvation goodbye.

For conservative Christians who affirm the doctrine of inerrancy, the authority of the Bible mandates traditional belief in the virgin birth. As Albert Mohler puts it, "If Jesus was not born of the virgin then the Bible cannot be trusted when it comes to telling us the story of Jesus, and that mistrust cannot be limited to how he came to us in terms of the incarnation."[3] On the assumptions of inerrancy, everything written in the Bible—unless blatantly indicated otherwise by the text's genre (i.e., poetry or parables)—must be taken as straightforward and historical. As the ole' fundamentalist saying goes, "The Bible is perfect, from the Table of Contents to the maps."

Conservatives argue that the denial of the virgin birth inevitably leads to a denial of the divinity of Jesus. Mohler insists that this doctrine anchors Christianity because the incarnation and divinity of Jesus depend on it: "The fact is that biblical Christianity and ultimately the Gospel of Christ cannot survive the denial of the virgin birth. Because without the virgin birth, you end up with a very different Jesus than the fully human, fully divine savior revealed in scripture."[4]

For many conservatives, belief in the virginal conception guarantees Jesus's divine origin and his unique divine-human nature.[5] They insist that God needed a miraculous, virginal conception to bring about the incarnation of the divine Son of God in human form. As another of Stanley's critics puts it, "If his birth were like any other human birth—through the union of a human father and mother—we would question his full divinity."[6] But there's no obvious reason why the entrance of the Son of God into the world had to be a spectacular, supernatural event. Their worry reveals a surprisingly limited view of God, who apparently requires the mechanism of virginal conception to pull off the feat of incarnation. Or at the very least, their God needs a grand entrance.

The irony is thick. Many conservative Christians resist any suggestions that God is limited; they don't like to imagine a God constrained by external circumstances. The fundamentalist catalog of God's attributes usually includes unlimited power. So, it's odd to read conservatives insisting that God needed a virginal conception to fully enter creation and become a human being.

There's another problem with the conservative response: They put the focus of the incarnation and the divinity of Jesus onto a single biological and historical moment, at the point of the origin of Jesus's human life. They insist that here, at the precise moment of conception, God introduced divinity into human nature. But as Andrew Lincoln rightly argues, when we think about the incarnation, we shouldn't limit our attention to the conception or birth of Jesus; rather, we should consider the overall "pattern of his life" as portrayed in the Gospels.[7] The incarnation of God in Jesus encompasses the duration of his life and ministry. His divinity doesn't depend upon a miraculous conception. Nor does his divinity overshadow his humanity.

THE LEGO JESUS

Two Christmases ago, my daughter Ella received an imitation LEGO princess set. After she opened the set and put together the pieces, she tried to integrate her new imitation set with genuine LEGO blocks. The venture was frustrating for both her and me as we struggled unsuccessfully to fit pieces together that just weren't made for each other.

"But Dad, why can't you make it work?"

"I just can't, sweetie. These pieces aren't meant to go together."

If you think it's hard to snap imitation "Lego" and genuine LEGO together, try fitting a divine nature and a human nature together in one person.

In 451 CE, over 500 bishops and theologians met at the Council of Chalcedon to determine what should be affirmed and what should be denied about the person Jesus Christ. This meeting of minds resulted in the "Definition" of Chalcedon, which insisted that Jesus is both fully divine and fully human. They neglected to explain *how* the two natures come together in Jesus. (Thanks for nothing, crusty old theologians!)

The council did, however, proclaim two then-common understandings of Jesus to be heretical: (1) Docetism, which emphasized Jesus's divinity at the expense of his humanity, and (2) Adoptionism, which accentuated Jesus's humanity and minimized his divinity. Some Adoptionists believed the divine Son of God chose the human person Jesus of Nazareth and borrowed (adopted) his human body for a time and purpose.[8] Within that group, some believed that the Son of God descended upon Jesus of Nazareth at his baptism or resurrection; others believed that Jesus was simply a human being chosen by God to be the Messiah because of his piety and devotion. Whatever the variety, Adoptionists had this belief in common: Jesus wasn't—and isn't—equal to the divine Son of God.

The council intended to rule out both errors: Docetism's divine (but not truly human) Jesus and Adoptionism's human (but not truly divine) Jesus. Chalcedon insisted that Jesus was both fully divine and fully human, but as one, integrated person. The two natures fit together in a flawless, seamless whole, "without division," "without confusion," and "without contradiction."

It took nearly a month for these theologians to come up with this "Definition." Perhaps they should have stayed another month! It's one thing to assert the "two natures," another thing to work out its implications. Even today, many thoughtful Christians try to figure out how divine omniscience coheres with a Jesus limited in knowledge (Mark 13:32). They wonder how a God immune to sin and temptation (James 1:13) could be tempted (Hebrews 4:15). Some ask how the divine Son could experience deep emotional and spiritual struggle in the Garden of Gethsemane (Matthew 26:36–46). And they wonder how, if Jesus was truly divine, his will could differ from God's will (Luke 22:42). They ponder how boundless, container-less divinity can be confined to a physical, human body.

But despite the frustrations, theologians continue to wrangle the divinity and humanity together, like Ella and me trying to snap together imitation and genuine LEGO blocks. The problem stems in part from an outdated understanding of the human person. For much of history, theologians assumed that human beings are composed of two *substances*, one material (the body) and the other immaterial—defined as the soul, the spirit, or even the mind.[9] So these theologians couldn't figure out how to fit the body and the soul together with the divine and human natures in Jesus. I can't blame them: it makes my head spin! And the effort only contributes to a disjointed, schizophrenic portrait of Jesus; divine in some ways, human in others. Divine sometimes, human at others.

That problem is history—or should be, anyway.

Wolfhart Pannenberg explains that faulty assumptions about human nature lay behind these frustrated attempts to synthesize divinity and humanity in Jesus. As he puts it, "The problem results from speaking of 'two' natures as if they were on the same plane."[10] But divinity and humanity aren't two distinct but comparable substances that exist side by side. They aren't like peanut butter and chocolate combined into a candy bar (e.g., Reeses). Nor are they two distinct physical things, like genuine LEGO blocks and the knockoff variety, that frustrate attempts to piece them together. Divinity is of a different kind altogether than humanity. The integrity of humanity isn't violated when divinity makes its home there.

Similarly, Kathryn Tanner proposes that the difference between divinity and humanity may be, ironically enough, what makes the incarnation work.[11] The infinite doesn't compete against or conflict with the finite, because they differ in kind. God's transcendence means God can and does enter creation without conflict—without competing against it or doing violence to it. Rather than think of Jesus's divinity and humanity in "terms of isolable, discrete qualities" (which seem impossible to fit together) we should think of divinity and humanity as overall descriptions of Jesus's life—while acknowledging that they constitute "different levels or planes of reality."[12] The Son of God can become Jesus of Nazareth; his humanity remains genuine humanity for the duration of his incarnate life, from conception to resurrection.

Divinity isn't a substance that can be analyzed under a microscope or genetically coded. It's not a "thing" that entered in Jesus. But Christians who want to continue to affirm, along with Chalcedon, the two natures of Christ can do so even while moving beyond belief in the virgin birth. They can simply affirm that the synthesis of the divine and human natures occurred by the power of God right at the very moment of conception; a conception that resulted from sexual intercourse between a mother and a father. They could also affirm that God ordained the human conception of Jesus to bring about the redemption of the world.

The theological intentions of the creeds do not

necessitate that we believe in a miraculous, virginal conception. If God can work providentially through natural processes, the birth of the Son of God could just as easily have been triggered by human sex. Many questions remain, of course, since the problem raised by the unity of the eternal divine Son of God and the localized, historical human person Jesus of Nazareth is complicated, just like the question whether Jesus was really born of a virgin.

THE JESUS WHO PRAYED AND PUKED

In 1988, Martin Scorsese released *The Last Temptation of Christ*, a film that depicted Jesus in a psychological and spiritual struggle between will and desire. The movie explores Jesus's struggle with his own identity as he works through anxiety, fear, depression, anger, desire, and disappointment. He desperately tries to understand the voice speaking to him—unsure whether it's God, Satan, or just tricks of his own mind.

Jesus confronts a variety of temptations and on the road to the cross he faces his "last temptation." He could walk away from the pain, the scorn, and the death by refusing his divinely appointed mission to die on the cross for humanity. He could take up a normal human life of love, family life, and fulfilled erotic desire. He could decline his Father's will, marry Mary Magdalene, and find happiness in a long, human life.

The film is based on the 1955 novel by Nikos Kazantzakis, which explored the implications of the full humanity of Jesus. Neither the film nor the novel concludes that Jesus yielded to temptation. The point was that dealing with real temptation as a human being means facing at times excruciating psychological, emotional, and spiritual challenges. As a true human being, Jesus's divine identity did not shield him from struggle, whether physical or existential.

The release of the novel resulted in high-level condemnation: the Vatican denounced it and the Greek Orthodox Church tried to ban it. The release of the film resulted in protests wherever it was shown. Their reactions recall our earlier discussion of the sacred. The hint of any real psychological and emotional vulnerability in Jesus elicits anxiety and condemnation. But their most vexing concern seems to have been with the film's portrayal of sexuality: The divine Son of God in the person of Jesus of Nazareth had erotic feelings, was vulnerable to sensual desire, and genuinely faced sexual temptation. But traditionalists who balk at the notion must contend with the letter to the Hebrews: "For we do not have a high priest who is unable to sympathize with our weaknesses, but we have one who in every respect has been tested as we are, yet without sin" (Hebrews 4:15). Traditional Christianity tends to focus on the phrase, "without sin," and minimizes the second part: "in every respect" and "tested as we are."

When I taught a Christology course at a conservative evangelical seminary, I showed clips from the film. My goal was to offer students a chance to reflect on Jesus's humanity and how he might have developed as a person in those decades of his life we know nothing about. It's reasonable to imagine that "every respect" includes: struggles, sickness, eccentricities of personality, pet peeves, anxieties, accidents, disappointments, fears, desires, regrets, loves, and on and on.

My family and I attend a theologically diverse and moderate Protestant church. We recite the Apostles' Creed every week. We sing traditional hymns and at Christmastime, songs filled with references to Mary and to the virgin birth. I led a Bible study in my church on the topic as I was writing this book. I was fully aware of the variety of theological perspectives represented in this congregation and was not surprised at the mixed responses to my thesis.

When I first suggested the possibility that perhaps we should no longer read the Gospel accounts of the virgin birth literally, several heads were visibly shaking with anxious disapproval, while others seemed happy to hear an alternative, progressive option. As I began to lay out my case for moving beyond a literal virgin birth, I mentioned in passing that Jesus Christ, the incarnate Son of God, experienced human life like the rest of us, which surely included not just emotions, but all types of human experiences, including contracting illnesses. One earnest congregant exclaimed with surprise, "Jesus got sick? How could he? He was God!"

That question underscored the challenge that lay before me: Since many Christians haven't come to terms with the logic of the incarnation, how could I make a compelling case for the human conception of Jesus based on that logic? I was tempted to show a clip from *The Last Temptation of Christ*. I refrained, probably wisely.

I find it hard to believe that anyone has lived into adulthood without getting physically sick, Jesus included. Yes, Jesus was a man of prayer. But he was also a man who puked.

THE DEEP DIVE OF THE DIVINE SON OF GOD

At the heart of the idea of the incarnation lies the biblical teaching that the eternal, divine Son of God "emptied himself," being "born in human likeness," and "being found in human form" (Philippians 2:7–8). This emptying (*kenosis*) means that the divine Son of God embraced creation as one of it, relinquishing the prerogatives of divinity. The boundless, physically limitless logos became a real, individual, human being: flesh, blood, bone, brain, and all. The Word of God accepted the limitations and frailties of the human body, when he was conceived in Mary.

Kenosis, or self-emptying, best answers the question how Jesus of Nazareth could also be the divine Son of God. In the incarnation, the eternal, divine Son dives deep into creation and is born as Jesus of Nazareth—fully human and fully divine, without contradiction. Because divinity doesn't conflict with humanity, the divine eternal Son doesn't overwhelm or undermine the humanity when he becomes zygote Jesus and eventually the crucified Messiah.

Conceived in Mary, the Son of God takes up residence with us, *as one of us*. In the incarnation, the Son of God underwent a kind of transformation when he entered history and was born as Jesus of Nazareth. Nonetheless, Jesus did not cease being divine; he remained the Word, Wisdom, and in later theological language: the second person of the Trinity. This is the biggest difference between Jesus and the rest of us: Jesus of Nazareth was the divine Son of God as a human being. We aren't.

But the point of the incarnation was not to shame us or to leave us to our own devices; rather, Jesus shows us a better way to be human—and helps us, too.

THE SPIRIT GUIDED HIM

Jesus enjoyed a deep, abiding union with the Father and with the Spirit. The Gospels speak of the closeness of the Spirit to and with Jesus from the beginning of his life. The Spirit was there; the Spirit was active; the Spirit was uniquely and intensely present. In the biblical narratives, the Spirit actively participates in the life of Jesus soon after the conception, leading Jesus into the wilderness of temptation and descending upon Jesus at his baptism—marking his vocation as the Christ (Messiah) with the visible blessing of God. Jesus's close relation to the Spirit is also indicated by his promise to the disciples that the Spirit will be the form of his (Jesus's) presence to them, following his death and resurrection.

As the self-emptying incarnate Son of God, Jesus had a unique relationship with God the Father and with the Holy Spirit. The high priestly prayer (John 17:1–26) indicates Jesus's close relation to both the Father and the Spirit as well as his desire that his disciples would emulate and aspire toward that same union. When we think of the divinity of Jesus, we should simultaneously think of the Spirit and the Father. And we should desire deeper intimacy, or union, with God and with our fellow divine image-bearers.

I admit there's a paradox here: Jesus was truly and fully human, and yet, as the preexistent Son of God in incarnational form, his relations with the Godhead (Father and Spirit) were intensified beyond our typical experiences of God. But a theology of *kenosis* insists Jesus didn't enter life fully equipped to understand everything about God, his own identity as Messiah and Son of God, or his vocation in the world. It's not like the Matrix: he didn't take the "red pill" and subsequently have all requisite (divine) knowledge downloaded into his brain. Rather, the Gospel of Luke tells us he "increased in wisdom and in years, and in divine and human favor" (Luke 2:52). Jesus's consciousness of his vocation and identity develops over time through the course of his life. God confirms the uniqueness of Jesus's person and role in salvation history by raising him from the dead.

Jesus was truly human and therefore not separate *in kind* from us. Nonetheless, we should also happily admit his uniqueness. Jesus Christ came to "save the lost" (Luke 19:10), to reconcile us to God and to each other, and to call us into Kingdom life. Jesus invites us even now to intimacy with God—with the Father, with the Spirit, and with the Son—adopted as children of God and siblings of Christ.

The miracle of the incarnation pronounces and enacts this invitation. The Son of God became human not by bypassing or diverting the processes of human life. Rather, he became human *through humanity* from the very beginning of his early life: by procreation from human parents, from conception to culmination, in his resurrection from the dead.

DEMENTIA, RESURRECTION, AND HOPE

I was expecting the phone call. We had recently moved my mother into a memory care facility. Not long after that emotionally painful transition, my mom woke up in the middle of the night, wandered in her room and fell, hitting her head. (Dementia didn't just steal her memory, but her coordination, too.) She had a pretty bad gash and was taken to an emergency room. That was the beginning of a very fast decline. When my dad phoned me a few weeks later, I knew what was coming. We were near the end. I headed to Wisconsin and to her bedside.

Alzheimer's doesn't kill you directly. It steals your capacities and eventually, your will to live. By the end, my mom's body was starving itself. Hospice staff makes everything as comfortable as possible, but it's heart-wrenching to see your own flesh and blood, your own mother, deteriorate. There's nothing she could do about it. There's nothing anyone could do about it.

The CD player on the nightstand piped classical music, her favorite. Mom was an accomplished pianist with a lifetime of practice, several compositions to her name, and countless performances in church and other venues.

The music had been the last thing to go. Soon after we moved her to the care facility, she'd wander the hallways, singing simple but beautiful melodies, hints of songs long past.

The singing had stopped. Now there was just breathing—heavy and steady. Unmusical notes, signals of a beautiful life near the end.

As I took my place by her bedside, I could swear her eyes lit up for a second—a brief instant of recognition amid a haze of unknowing. Lost memories. Distant names and faces blurred into nothing. Her already-thin body was now frail as could be. The disease is steady and unrelenting. Plaques in her brain had degenerated her cells, resulting in loss of memory, inability to walk or stand safely, disconnection from the social world.

The incarnation was for my mom. Not only for my mom, of course, but for her nonetheless. The Son of God assumed human nature. God took on flesh, bone, blood, brain, and DNA. Jesus made memories—and lost them, too. The Son of God embraced the frailty and beauty of our precarious existence. The life of Jesus shows us that our bodies are good and that creation is God's gift. *We* are God's gift. Although our bodies will not last forever in their current form, they are precious still.

The thought of the incarnation takes me now to my mom, lying in her bed in her final days. It really matters that the conception of Jesus was a truly and fully human one. It matters that Jesus was not some hybrid divine-human person, an interruption of the human species, a superhero with a different physical or genetic composition from you and me. God entered our species—a species that faces unending trials and that creates plenty of our own. Whether physical diseases or psychological illness; whether uncontrollable situations of life, causing anxiety and pain; whether social conflicts like racism, sexism, and violence of all sorts. God did not avoid our body, our genetics, our brain, our human condition—individual and social. He entered them deeply and fully in Jesus.

At some point, every person must come to terms with the certainty of death.[13] We share with all creatures the instinct to avoid immediate dangers, whether perceived or real. But we carry a unique capacity and burden to conceptualize and imagine our future demise as inevitable. We philosophize about it. We pour resources into staving it off. We develop sophisticated medicines and technologies to delay its coming. But nonetheless, it comes—and we often despair of its power over our defenses.

A fully human conception of Jesus matters because of the inevitability of death. Jesus entered our human species in a normal way and lived a fully human life; he understood the anxiety that comes with mortality. The Garden of Gethsemane tells this story. He experienced deep grief at the awareness of his coming suffering and death (Matthew 26:37–38). Nonetheless, he drank the cup of sorrow, believing that God would transform his suffering and overcome death's power. Jesus embraced mortality by accepting the cross: "your will be done" (Matthew 26:42).

The incarnation is God's affirmation of the goodness of creation. But it's also God's promise to redeem humanity; to heal us—and all of creation. Paul says, "We know that the whole creation has been groaning in labor pains until now; and not only the creation, but we ourselves, who have the first fruits of the Spirit, groan inwardly while we wait for adoption, the redemption of our bodies (Romans 8:22–23). Do you hear the resonance there? The groaning of creation . . . "in labor pains." Jesus came into the world through the labor of real, physical, human birth. And through human conception, too. He became us in every way, so he can heal us in every way.

At the close of Mom's funeral, I read my favorite passage:

Then I saw a new heaven and a new earth; for the first heaven and the first earth had passed away, and the sea was no more. And I saw the holy city, the new Jerusalem, coming down out of heaven from God, prepared as a bride adorned for her husband. And I heard a loud voice from the throne saying,

"See, the home of God is among mortals.
He will dwell with them;
they will be his peoples,
and God himself will be with them;
he will wipe every tear from their eyes.
Death will be no more;
mourning and crying and pain will be no more,
for the first things have passed away." (Revelation
21:1–4)

I barely made it through the reading. I choked up imagining a day when my mom's deteriorated brain would be renewed or replaced. Her memories restored. Her relationships rejuvenated. Her creativity back, her music returned to her fingers. And her mind, her joy, her *self* alive again.

The hope of the resurrection and of the new creation is based on the promise of God coming down and living among us, with us. It's based in the value of embodiment, of flesh and blood, of vibrant, tangible, created life. As another translation (NIV) puts it, "God's dwelling place is now among the people, and he will dwell with them" (Revelation 21:3). The fulfillment of this promise began with the incarnation, when the Son of God became Jesus of

Nazareth. God lived with the people—and was one of us, too.

The virgin birth is not the pillar of the Christian faith. That distinction is reserved for the resurrection. Belief in the resurrection of Jesus galvanized the early Christians, forming a movement around the person, teachings, and work of Jesus Christ. Christians affirm that the resurrection of Jesus is an event that precipitates and foreshadows our own experience of resurrection from death. In the raising of Christ from the grave, the final power of death was overcome. Death lost its sting. Resurrection hope enables believers to live in anticipation of that ultimate overcoming.

When I stated my belief in a physical resurrection to a graduate theology student, he came at me hard—wanting to catch me in a theological trap: "How can you treat the virgin birth as a legend but take the resurrection so seriously—even literally? Why reject one miracle, but accept the other?"

It's a fair enough point. Sure, I can mess with the manger scene (and with yours), but don't go messing with my empty tomb!

The eager graduate student equates belief in the virgin birth with belief in the resurrection; then he concludes that I can't reject the one without rejecting the other. True: both beliefs involve the assumption of supernatural divine intervention —that God can change the course of history, of biology, of creation. But when all is said and done, that's not my problem with the virgin birth. The *primary* (but not only) problem is that it conflicts with the logic of the incarnation, the very basis of the gospel itself. A virginal conception is *internally* incoherent with the proclamation that God became a human being in Jesus. A virgin birth gives us a different Christ than the one we really need.

Furthermore, the virgin birth and the resurrection differ in an important respect. Traditional Christianity proclaims the singularity of the virginal conception: it happened only once in history and only to one person. This renders Jesus not just unique, but a different kind of human being from the rest of us—a new species, a divine-human hybrid. The resurrection, on the other hand, will happen to *all of us*, to all human beings.

Paul describes Jesus's resurrection as the "first fruits" (1 Corinthians 15:23) of an eventual transformation that all the redeemed will experience by the grace of God. Our hope in the resurrection doesn't rely on current science, anthropology, or history—or even anecdotal evidence. We sure don't get that hope from the news and from social media. It comes from God's promise that through the resurrection of Christ, death doesn't have the final say.

Robert Russell suggests that the resurrection of Jesus reflects the possibility of a transformation of the laws of nature—pointing to the possibility of a future new creation based on a new organization of nature.[14] We may have a pretty good sense of how things work *now* and of how they have worked in the past, but present knowledge doesn't necessarily rule out a God who does new things—perhaps even transforming physics, cosmology, and biology. Science describes nature and its processes, but it doesn't *prescribe* or determine what may or may not happen in the future—especially if God is truly creator, provider, and redeemer.[15]

On this basis, if the idea of a virginal conception cohered with the incarnation and with the gospel, I would be more inclined to embrace it. Many believers see the virgin birth as a testimony to a God who can intervene in nature and biology to bring about a remarkable result. But the cumulative case convinces me that Christians are better off moving beyond the virgin birth and fixing their hope on the incarnation and in the resurrection.

Jürgen Moltmann sees the resurrection as central to Christian faith because "the faith of the New Testament has its foundation in the testimony to

Christ's resurrection."[16] The resurrection represents the culmination of the incarnation, while the virgin birth stands outside of and runs against its logic. In an ultimate sense, the virgin birth offers neither hope nor healing. The resurrection offers both.

Jesus is the healer, the liberator, the revealer, the savior, the incarnate Emmanuel. Jesus is much more besides, but as the incarnate Son of God, he represented God's love in the world, and he enjoyed a regular, intimate communion with the Father and the Spirit; communion that remains aspirational for the rest of us as we hope for the resurrection and work toward the kingdom of God on earth.

STANDING, SINGING, RECITING

Many Christian hymnals today include a hymn, "Savior of the Nations Come," the lyrics of which were written by the medieval theologian, Ambrose of Milan, and subsequently translated by Martin Luther in the sixteenth century. The first three verses exemplify a gnostic view of Jesus. The assumption that Jesus's origin had to have been supernatural betrays a fundamental suspicion that human nature was beneath God's dignity. Jesus simply *had* to come from God and *not* from or through the indignity of natural, human procreation.

Savior of the nations, come,
Virgin's Son, make here Thy home!
Marvel now, O heaven and earth,
That the Lord chose such a birth.

Not by human flesh and blood,
By the Spirit of our God,
Was the Word of God made flesh—
Woman's Offspring, pure and fresh.

Wondrous birth! O wondrous Child
Of the Virgin undefiled!
Though by all the world disowned,
Still to be in heaven enthroned.

With all due deference to theological greats like Anselm and Luther, I'm tempted to rewrite the hymn, and especially the second verse. The line "by the Spirit of our God" doesn't conflict with "by human flesh and blood." The Word of God might well have been the offspring of fully human flesh, both of a man and of a woman. Why not? Were Jesus the offspring of human sexual procreation, the Spirit of God would have been no less intimately present to the conception, no less providentially involved in the human origin of the divine Son of

God. And we could still sing the final verse with gusto:

Praise to God the Father sing,
Praise to God the Son, our King,
Praise to God the Spirit be
Ever and eternally.

When I sing in church old hymns like this one and when I recite the phrase "born of the virgin" with my community, I'm taking my place as a willing, committed participant in the church universal. Some stanzas of hymns resonate in me more than others. Some lines of a creed ring truer than others, given all that we know now. But I sing nonetheless and I continue to speak the language and story of the historic faith. In my reciting of a creed or confession, I acknowledge I'm a part of a wider community that is informed by a biblical and theological story; one rich in depth and broad in diversity, the depth and breadth of which can't be fully represented by the voicing of a single creed or by the singing of a single hymn.

My manger scene has changed, but it's still there. And Jesus is no less at its center. The baby is in the manger. And the baby is truly human, but no less divine. Rethinking the virgin birth along the lines of a theology of incarnation means that God brings beauty out of scandal and salvation out of brokenness. God dives deep into creation and Jesus crosses boundaries to spark salvation, healing, and reconciliation for the world. And God very well may use the most ordinary or even scandalous events to bring about the most extraordinary results.

NOTES

1. Cited in http://politics.blog.ajc.com/2016/12/27/dont-believe-in-jesus-virgin-birth-not-a-problem-says-andy-stanley/.

2. https://www.washingtonpost.com/news/acts-of-faith/wp/2016/12/24/megachurch-pastor-ignites-debate-after-suggesting-christianity-doesnt-hinge-on-jesus-birth/?utm_term=.7afodbabo9dd.

3. Ibid.

4. Ibid.

5. Ibid.

6. Ibid.

7. Andrew Lincoln, *Born of a Virgin? Reconceiving Jesus in the Bible, Tradition, and Theology* (Grand Rapids, MI: Eerdmans, 2013), 279.

8. Wolfhart Pannenberg, *Jesus – God and Man*, 2nd edition (Louisville: Westminster John Knox, 1977), 150.

9. F. LeRon Shults, *Christology and Science* (Grand Rapids, MI: Eerdmans, 2008), 31–38.

10. Pannenberg, *Jesus – God and Man*, 322. See also Shults, *Christology and Science*, 56–57.

11. Kathyrn Tanner, *Jesus, Humanity, and the Trinity* (Minneapolis: Fortress Press, 2001), 11–16. See also the discussion of Tanner on this point in Celia Deane-Drummond, *Christ and Evolution: Wonder and Wisdom* (Minneapolis: Fortress Press, 2009), 96–100.

12. Tanner, *Jesus, Humanity, and the Trinity*, 16.

13. For a sustained treatment of humanity's awareness of death and the anxiety it creates, see Ernest Becker, *The Denial of Death* (New York: Free Press, 1973).

14. Robert John Russell, *Cosmology: From Alpha to Omega* (Minneapolis: Fortress Press, 2008), 298–327.

15. Russell, *Cosmology*, 308–9.

16. Jürgen Moltmann, *The Way of Jesus Christ: Christology in Messianic Dimensions* (Minneapolis: Fortress Press, 1995), 79.

CONCLUSION: A MORE HUMAN GOD

In 1995, Joan Osborne released "One of Us," a song (written by Eric Bazillion) that probably made a lot of top-forty radio-listening Christians uncomfortable. The lyrics imagine the shocking possibility that "God was one of us." Perhaps a "slob" like us and a "stranger on a bus" just trying to get home.

The image of God as a slob pricks at the sense of the sacred that most of us have when thinking about the divine Creator of the universe. But the incarnation brings the eternal, divine Son of God into our own experience in a radical and tangible way. Think about it: Maybe Jesus kept a messy room. Maybe he sometimes forgot names and showed up late to appointments. Maybe, as a young teenager, he got an erection while holding a girl's—or boy's—hand, and maybe he didn't know what was happening. Maybe he got picked last for the team, or was bullied a lot as a kid. Maybe he had diarrhea as an adult once and had an accident. Maybe people saw it—or smelt it. Maybe Jesus had a lisp, or a limp. Perhaps Jesus was a mediocre carpenter, but he still loved his work.

If Jesus was clumsy, or daydreamed a little too much, or wasn't physically attractive, would that make you worship him any less? Would your redemption be less significant? Would his resurrection from the dead no longer matter to you?

I'm not being disrespectful here. But consider that Jesus of Nazareth, the incarnate Son of God, was a lot more like you and me than we ever imagined.

The song's question, "What if God was one of us?" illustrates the radical, dramatic, paradoxical notion that the eternal God becomes a human being—a real flesh, blood, bone, and brain person in a historical time and place. If God had a "face," what would that face look like? Of course, it doesn't really matter what Jesus's face really looked like. But it matters that he had one; it matters that he was one of us—in every way.

Moving beyond a miraculous, virginal conception really matters. Here's how:

KYLE ROBERTS

WE CAN ACCEPT THE HUMANITY
OF THE BIBLE

Accepting a fully human incarnation allows us to
embrace not just the humanity of Jesus, but the
humanity of the Bible, too. We can accept that the
Bible includes historical contradictions and theological ambiguities. The Bible is a compiled library; it's
a diverse collection of histories, poetry, laws, letters,
and legends—each witnessing in its own way to the
power and love of God. We can therefore read the
two infancy narratives, with all their conflicting
details and historical problems, through the lens of
a more nuanced view of biblical authority than the
doctrine of inerrancy provides. The infancy narratives serve as theologically motivated constructions
of the divine origin of the Son of God in the flesh.
But the New Testament contains other reflections
on the uniqueness of Jesus, too—based not in a virgin birth but in the preexistence of the divine Son as
logos, or Word of God.

The earliest witnesses to the life of Jesus (Paul
and Mark) apparently knew nothing of a virginal
conception, and there may be hints of a scandalous
conception, too. Of all the biblical authors, Paul and
John were most invested in the theme of the incarnation but they had no awareness of or use for a virgin

192

birth story. By moving beyond the traditional theology of the virgin birth, we can still affirm the Bible's uniqueness and power as the Spirit-inspired word of God. But we can also relate to the Bible in a more human—and more meaningful—way.

WE CAN EMBRACE SCIENCE AS A SOURCE FOR THEOLOGY

If we take science seriously, it's difficult to accept a virginal conception as the mechanism for the incarnation. This isn't because science rules out miracles. I don't accept that notion, and I doubt you do, either. But we know a lot more about human biology, conception, and procreation than the biblical authors and the early Christian theologians did. Our theological beliefs are always intertwined with our assumptions about how the world works (which is the domain of science). And that's okay. But it means we should be open to evaluating our inherited theological beliefs as our assumptions change about the world—and about ourselves.

In the case of the virginal conception, contemporary biology suggests that the notion of a virginal conception—resulting in the birth of the *male* human Jesus of Nazareth—is not just complicated, but contradictory. Not only does the possibility require extensive conceptual gymnastics to sort out, but the notion of a virginal conception undermines the very point of the incarnation—that Jesus became a true human being. Because science helps us understand what human beings are, that insight should factor into our evaluation of the virgin birth.

WE CAN AFFIRM THE GOODNESS OF CREATION AND SEXUALITY

Some early theologians rejected the idea of a bloodless and painless birth of Jesus (virginity *during* the birth) because it diminished the incarnation and undermined the value of creation. They rightly insisted the Son of God did not shy away from the realities of the physical, human experience, but allowed himself to be born into that world—as a part of that world. The physical birth of Jesus testifies to God's love for creation and to God's affirmation that creation is good. On the same logic, a human conception of Jesus affirms the goodness of humanity as part of God's creation. The Son of God entered our world completely and unashamedly. He entered our humanity as one of us—not bypassing the evolution of our species, but joining the evolutionary line; sharing our body, our blood, our DNA.

A human conception also affirms the goodness

and beauty of human sexuality. God didn't circumvent human intercourse to initiate an incarnation, but used it to bring about the redemption of humanity and of the cosmos through Jesus Christ. A nonvirginal womb was no less appropriate for the divine Son of God than a virginal one. Furthermore, God didn't disregard the biological role of the male in the fertilization of the zygote Jesus of Nazareth. Accepting a human conception suggests that covenantal, erotic love assumes a significant place in Christian discipleship, alongside and not inferior to the religious vocation of lifelong chastity.

GOD EMPATHIZES WITH OUR CONDITION AND TRANSFORMS IT

A human conception testifies that God did not stand apart from our world or aloof from our human experience, but entered it fully in Jesus of Nazareth. He *became* it by becoming one of us. He took on our flesh, our body, our blood, our brain, our DNA. He experienced life as a true human being: loneliness and friendship, happiness and tragedy, confusion and delight. He knew rejection and friendship, success and regret, joy and sorrow. He understood the love of life and the fear of death. God loves us more than we ever thought possible and identifies with our humanity, because the Son of God was one of us.

But empathy isn't everything. The incarnation also means God transforms our condition. The Son of God became human so he could heal humanity and *all* of creation. The Word entered the world and the universe to redeem it from within. The divine empathy enabled by the incarnation culminates in the transformation of creation toward the will of God. The kingdom comes—and is coming still. Creation awaits new creation, a restoration that began in a fully human incarnation. The Son of God didn't become Jesus of Nazareth to shame us, but to save us. Redemption is made possible and actual through the cross and the resurrection.

JESUS SHOWS US A BETTER WAY TO BE HUMAN

Only God can finally and fully bring the kingdom. But we dare not relegate the work of justice and of redemption to God alone. Through the incarnation, Jesus empathizes with us and empowers us to live in accordance with God's will in the world. But he also reveals to us a better way to be human. Jesus teaches us and shows us how to be living illustrations of the kingdom that's on its way. A human conception means that the Jesus who showed us a better way, and who calls us to that better way, was also *like us in every way.*

The incarnation means the divine Son of God became the person Jesus of Nazareth at a place and time in history, in first-century Galilee and Jerusalem. God didn't disrupt the evolutionary line to redeem humanity and creation. Rather, in and through the very stuff of humanity—our human species—God manifests salvation, offers forgiveness, and opens wide the possibility for reconciliation and for absolute healing through the hope of resurrection.

While you and I will never be the divine Son of God, the logos, the Word and Wisdom of God, we are nonetheless invited into intimacy with God as sons and daughters, reconciled with God, with each other, and with all creation. Deep and tangible communion with God and with our fellow human beings, through fellowship with Jesus, Father, and Spirit, is possible.

A HUMAN CONCEPTION GIVES US A MORE HUMAN MARY

God affirms the equality of both male and female. An incarnation by natural conception affirms the inherent goodness of both sexes. It discourages us from allocating special responsibility to the male as the distributor of original sin. It precludes us from assigning special virtue or vice to female sexuality. And a human conception of Jesus inspires us to value Mary for more than her sexuality (or virginity) and her procreative capacity.

Rather, we should view Mary through the broader lens the Gospels give us: not only as receptive to God's will, but also as assertive and active in God's salvation history. As the God-bearer (*Theotokos*), Mary's motherhood needn't be diminished. But we should see her within the wider context expressed by the Magnificat—a Jewish peasant girl who seized an opportunity for a lead role in God's liberation of her people. Understanding Mary within the complex framework of human conception in the first century CE means we must be always sensitive to the tragedy and pervasiveness of violence against women and girls. And we must actively strain toward a more just and more peaceful world. A human conception implies the full inclusiveness of both sexes (and intersex, too) in the coming of God's kingdom on earth, as it is in heaven.

A FULL INCARNATION GIVES US A BETTER CHRISTIANITY

When Christians are given permission to question inherited beliefs like the virgin birth, this can open them up to a more ambiguous and complex, but also more mature faith. Acknowledging divisive theological doctrines as nonessential to Christian identity encourages humility about our beliefs—we can hold our beliefs more loosely. Collectively, it creates the potential for wider inclusion. The freedom to critically examine even the most cherished doctrines allows for more porous boundaries, both within our individual understandings of God and within communities of faith. More energy can be expended toward justice and less wasted on doctrinal gate-keeping. Or to use theological language, the emphasis shifts from *orthodoxy* (right thinking) to *orthopraxis* (right living). It's no secret that the doctrine of the virgin birth—like all the "fundamentals" of Christian orthodoxy—has been used as a political tool and an instrument of division, setting clear lines of demarcation of those who are included and those who are excluded.

Asking faithful questions can help decalcify hardened ideas and ideologies. Deconstruction of received theologies creates the potential for a humbler and deeper faith. Granted, this isn't an inevitable outcome. It can work the other way, too. And I don't offer my life as proof of either direction. But I will testify that the endeavor of asking critical and faithful questions of our inherited theologies has been, for me, a positively transforming experience.[1] I haven't lost faith; I feel that I've gone deeper in.

A FULL INCARNATION GIVES US A MORE HUMAN GOSPEL

Setting the notion of the virgin birth aside, and moving beyond a literal reading of the infancy narratives, allows us to feel more deeply and more powerfully the implications of God becoming one of us. The traditional theology of the virgin birth developed in an ancient time and place. It evidences a patriarchal view of sexuality and of femininity; it reflects an obviously outdated biology; it mirrors the practice of ancient cultures to valorize important leaders by giving them remarkable and supernatural origins. For me, though, the most poignant problem with the virgin birth regards the gospel itself: the good news that God came in the flesh in Jesus of Nazareth to reconcile the world and humanity.

A virginal conception undermines a deep and

consistent theology of the incarnation—the very basis of the gospel. If Jesus was fully human like you and me, his life began like yours and mine, via human conception. At the heart of it all, the point isn't to modernize the gospel, but to bring it back—to a more human origin.

The question of Mary's virginity matters because it affects how we practice Christian faith based on our understanding of the gospel. The gospel proclaims that Jesus was the Son of God as a human being. He advocated justice and righteousness. He denounced religious hypocrisy. He prayed for the kingdom of God. He conquered sin, death, and evil on the cross and was resurrected by God. And he invites us to come alongside of him now—as we live in anticipation of God's renewal of all things.

Accepting a human conception also gives us a more human God. The Son of God enters history and becomes a human being—not by a supernatural miracle that avoids the mechanism of intercourse but through the very stuff of human procreation. God makes room for genuine humanity to reflect God's own nature. God fully enters our world and our experience in Jesus of Nazareth, and God is *changed* by the incarnation.

I want my kids to read this book someday. I want a fully incarnate Son of God to shape their understanding of and practice of the Christian faith. A God who assumes our nature, our experience, and our struggle; who shows us a better way to be Christian and a better way to be human in the world.

Moving beyond belief in the virgin birth can enable relating to God with a greater sense of both mystery and wonder. We can affirm the goodness of creation and of humanity—while acknowledging its brokenness, too. Embracing the full incarnation opens new pathways for understanding Jesus Christ and for relating to God through him. Not altogether different, but a lot more human.

NOTES

1. For an explanation of the task of theology as critical reflection (deliberative theology) on our embedded beliefs (inherited theology), see Howard Stone and James Duke, *How to Think Theologically* (Minneapolis: Fortress Press, 2013).

ACKNOWLEDGMENTS

This book reflects the contributions of many people, both individuals and groups. I first want to thank my students at United Theological Seminary of the Twin Cities, who listened patiently as I talked through the arguments of the book, on more than one occasion. They offered substantive feedback and posed good, hard questions. I'm especially grateful to the students in my Senior Capstone Seminar for their pointed and poignant reflections. I'm also thankful for my warm-hearted, thoughtful friends in the adult education class at Colonial Church of Edina, Minnesota, who listened to my several presentations on the topics, and raised important questions. Some of the questions and stories from those interactions are included in this book.

Several individuals engaged me consistently in conversations about this topic at different points in this journey. Their friendship and collegiality have contributed greatly to the content and structure of this book, among them: Dr. Demian Wheeler, Dr.

Silas Morgan, Dr. Ken Reynhout, Dr. Paul Capetz, Sara Wilhelm Garbers, and Dan Addington. Several people took time to read and comment on chapters from the book, including my colleague, New Testament scholar Dr. Samuel Subramanian, who helped with issues pertaining to New Testament scholarship and biblical language. Two physicians, Dr. Richard Lussky and Dr. Brett Einerson, read several chapters and offered suggestions and corrections regarding medical content and terminology. Dr. Joy Doan, a biology professor, also provided poignant feedback on issues pertaining to genetics and evolution, resulting in a much stronger argument. My former colleague, Dr. Jeannine Brown, with whom I've recently written a commentary on the Gospel of Matthew (The Two Horizons Commentary Series, Eerdmans, forthcoming), also provided helpful feedback. My work with Jeannine on our other project has contributed greatly to my use of Matthew in this present book. I also want to thank my friends, Rachael and Joel Rydbeck, and my brother-in-law, Dan Addington, for allowing me to share a bit of their stories.

None of these friends and colleagues should be held accountable, either for the book's conclusion or for any other flaws in these pages.

Along with everyone involved on the Theology

for the People team at Fortress Press, I want to especially thank the editor, Dr. Tony Jones, both for inviting me to write this book and for his excellent editorial oversight and guidance. He's both pushed me and helped me in many ways to become a better writer and communicator. To the extent that I followed his suggestions, this book reflects his insistence that theology can be accessible and lively.

I'm deeply grateful to my wife, Sara, for her patience, love, and support. Writing a book is a time-consuming endeavor and often gets in the way of life. She's supported and encouraged me from the beginning to the final edits. And I must thank my two kids, Ella and Luke, for letting me share some stories about them in this book. They not only provided excellent diversions from the task of writing, they also increased the book's entertainment value!

Finally, to all those believers and seekers looking for a deeper way to think about Jesus, Mary, and what the birth of Christ means for us—I hope you've found something here in my journey, to help you in yours.